THE HIDDEN PLACES

# of Northumberland and Durham

Written by *Jo Noel-Stevens & Martin Stevens*

Foreword by ANGELA RIPPON

Acknowledgements

This book would not have been compiled without the dedicated help of the following : Zoe - Production, Elaine & Michelle - Administration, Sarah - Artist, and last but by no means least, Jo Noel-Stevens and Martin Stevens - Writing & Research.

All have contributed to what we hope is an interesting, useful and enjoyable publication.

OTHER TITLES IN THIS SERIES

The Hidden Places of North Yorkshire
The Hidden Places of Somerset, Avon & Dorset
The Hidden Places of Southern & Central Scotland
The Hidden Places of Yorkshire South, East and West
The Hidden Places of Nottinghamshire, Derbyshire & Lincolnshire
The Hidden Places of Oxfordshire, Buckinghamshire & Bedfordshire
The Hidden Places of Gloucestershire & Wiltshire
The Hidden Places of Hampshire & Isle of Wight
The hidden Places of Hereford & Worcester
The Hidden Places of Devon & Cornwall
The Hidden Places of Norfolk & Suffolk
The Hidden Places of Cumbria
The Hidden Places of Sussex

ISBN 1-871815-70-3
First Published in 1992

Tryfan House, Warwick Drive, Hale, Altrincham, Cheshire. WA15 9EA

Printed and bound in Great Britain by
The Guernsey Press Co. Ltd, Guernsey, Channel Islands.

Introduction

THE HIDDEN PLACES is designed to be an easily used book. Taking you in this instance, on a gentle meander through the beautiful countryside of Northumberland & Durham: however, our books cover many counties and will eventually encompass the whole of the United Kingdom. We have combined descriptions of the well-known and enduring tourist attractions with those more secluded and as yet little known venues, easy to miss unless you know exactly where you are going.

We include hotels, inns, restaurants, caravan parks and camping sites, historic houses, museums, gardens and general attractions throughout each of these fascinating counties: together with our research on the local history. For each attraction there is a line drawing and a brief description of the services offered. A map at the back of the book shows you exactly how to get to your destination and indicates the chapter relevant to each area. There is also a reference guide giving you full details of all the hotels, inns, etc., detailed.

We do not include firm prices or award merits. We merely wish to point out *The Hidden Places* that hopefully will improve your holiday or business trip and tempt you to return. The places featured in this book will we are sure, be pleased if you mention that it was *The Hidden Places* which prompted you to visit.

THE HIDDEN PLACES

of

Northumberland & Durham

Contents

Foreword

Chapter 1: Cleveland

Chapter 2: Central Durham

Chapter 3: Teesdale

Chapter 4: Weardale

Chapter 5: Tynedale

Chapter 6: Tyneside

Chapter 7: Central Northumberland

Chapter 8: The Northumberland Coast

Chapter 9: Berwick & The Border

Reference Guide

Foreword

How many times have you heard someone say "I don't know why we keep going abroad on holiday every year, when we haven't begun to explore or get to know our own country."

And it's true, Britain as a whole is full of the most wonderful countryside and coastline, and whether it is in the far west peninsular of Devon and Cornwall or in the Orkneys, we have some of the world's finest natural treasures. But it's the hidden nooks and crannies, the quiet places and the unexpected, that hold much of the true charm of any region.

Being a local helps, they have known about such places for generations. But the visitors may pass them by, and so miss many of the real pleasures.

So these books are by way of a privilege. Bringing you access to places, county by county, you may never have seen before. So enjoy, and perhaps understand why those of us fortunate enough to have been born here think of it as being God's own Kingdom.

ANGELA RIPPON

Cleveland

Kirkleatham Church

CHAPTER ONE

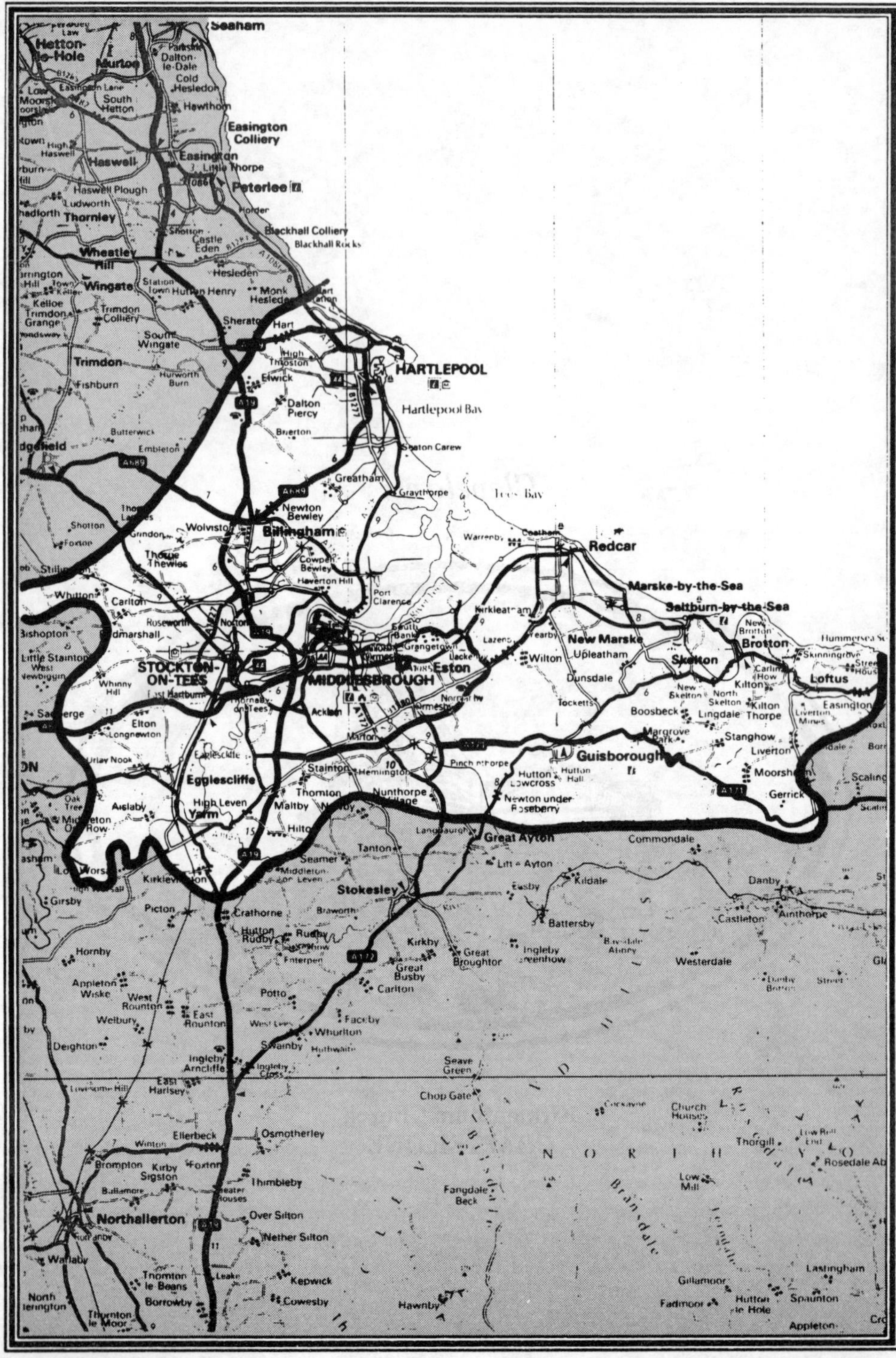

Seaham
Murton
Dalton-le-Dale
Cold Hesledon
South Hetton
Hawthorn
Easington Colliery
Haswell
Easington
Little Thorpe
Peterlee
Haswell Plough
Ludworth
Thornley
Horden
Shotton
Castle Eden
Blackhall Colliery
Blackhall Rocks
Wheatley Hill
Wingate
Hesleden
Hutton Henry
Monk Hesleden
Kelloe
Trimdon Grange
Trimdon Colliery
South Wingate
Hart
Trimdon
Fishburn
Hurworth Burn
High Throston
Elwick
HARTLEPOOL
Hartlepool Bay
Dalton Piercy
Butterwick
Brierton
Embleton
A689
A19
Seaton Carew
Greatham
Graythorpe
Tees Bay
Newton Bewley
Shotton
Foxton
Wolviston
Billingham
Grindon
Thorpe Thewles
Cowpen Bewley
Haverton Hill
Port Clarence
Warrenby
Coatham
Redcar
Marske-by-the-Sea
Saltburn-by-the-Sea
Whitton
Carlton
Roseworth
Norton
Kirkleatham
Redmarshall
Bishopton
Little Stainton
STOCKTON-ON-TEES
MIDDLESBROUGH
Grangetown
Eston
Wilton
Upleatham
New Marske
Skelton
Brotton
Loftus
Skinningrove
Whinny Hill
Dunsdale
Kilton
Kilton Thorpe
Boosbeck
Lingdale
North Skelton
New Skelton
Easington
Elton
Longnewton
Acklam
Tocketts
Margrove Park
Stanghow
Liverton
Liverton Mines
Guisborough
Moorsholm
Gerrick
Urlay Nook
Eaglescliffe
Egglescliffe
Stainton
Hemlington
Pinchinthorpe
Hutton Lowcross
Hutton Hall
Newton under Roseberry
Thornton
Nunthorpe Village
Aislaby
High Leven
Yarm
Maltby
Hilton
Great Ayton
Commondale
Middleton One Row
Tanton
Seamer
Little Ayton
Kildale
Danby
Ainthorpe
Castleton
Kirklevington
Middleton-on-Leven
Stokesley
Easby
Battersby
Girsby
Picton
Crathorne
Hutton Rudby
Rudby
Kirkby
Great Broughton
Ingleby Greenhow
Baysdale Abbey
Westerdale
Hornby
Appleton Wiske
Great Busby
Carlton
Danby Botton
West Rounton
East Rounton
Potto
Faceby
Welbury
Whorlton
Deighton
Swainby
Ingleby Arncliffe
Ingleby Cross
Seave Green
East Harlsey
Chop Gate
Church Houses
Ellerbeck
Osmotherley
Thorgill
Low Bell End
Rosedale Abbey
Brompton
Kirby Sigston
Foxton
Thimbleby
Low Mill
Fangdale Beck
N O R T H
Northallerton
Over Silton
Nether Silton
Thornton le Beans
Leake
Kepwick
Lastingham
Borrowby
Cowesby
Gillamoor
Hutton le Hole
Spaunton
Hawnby
Fadmoor
Thornton le Moor
Appleton

Chapter One - Map Reference Guide
Cleveland

Norman Conquest Hotel - Middlesborough

The Grand Hotel - Hartlepool

The Golden Eagle Hotel - Thornaby on Tees

The Sheraton Hotel - Stockton on Tees

Kirkleatham Old Hall - Kirkleatham

The Southern Cross Hotel - Marton

Street House Farm / Highcliffe Cottage - Loftus

Maltby Farm - Maltby

Leven Close Farm - High Leven

Castle Eden Walkway Country Park - Thorpe Thewles

Leo's Pub Club - Redcar

Claxton Hotel - Redcar

St Andrew's Church

CHAPTER ONE

Cleveland

Northumbria was the name of the ancient Anglo-Saxon kingdom established in northern England soon after the Romans departed. The kingdom literally included all the land in the North of England which lay 'north of the Humber' to the frequently changing Scottish border. It was this land which, after many invasions of Danes and Vikings, was ruled over by generations of ferocious warrior-kings until, in 960AD, their last prince, Eric Bloodaxe, was finally defeated at Rey Cross, at Stainmoor, on what is now the Cumbria boundary. Northumbria then became part of the larger kingdom of England, which was in turn subject to invasion and subjugation by the Normans in 1066.

The old name has survived, but does not cover quite as much territory as it did in early medieval times - Yorkshire has occupied much of the southern part for the last thousand years or so. Northumbria is now used as a name for England's four north-eastern counties - Cleveland, Durham, Tyne and Wear and Northumberland, each with an identity of its own.

Boundaries and politics apart, modern Northumbria contains some of the wildest, loneliest and most beautiful countryside in northern England, including the North Pennines and the Cheviots; a coastline of quite breathtaking beauty and splendour, dominated by a series of romantic castles; one of England's great cathedral cities built around perhaps the most noble English cathedral of them all; and, if that were not enough, two great modern industrial conurbations along the mouths of the Tyne and the Tees. This area boasts a cultural heritage that includes the early founding fathers of English Christianity and the builders of the first truly successful steam railways in the world.

But above all else, what will give any visitor to Northumbria warm and lasting memories is the people themselves - communities in towns as well as the countryside, whose hospitality, vigorous wit and sense of humour are legendary.

Cleveland is a relatively modern county, whose name is reflected by the long line of hills which run from the Vale of Mowbray to the coast, dividing the lower Tees Valley from the more rural North Yorkshire. Actually, though, the name of the region goes back to Anglo-Saxon times and means 'clay-lands', referring to the heavy soils and claybeds that overlie the relatively new, softer rocks of the rounded hills.

The county was created in 1974 from the former Borough of Teeside and parts of the old North Riding and County Durham. It includes the busy industrial towns around the mouth of the Tees - Stockton, Middlesborough, Hartlepool, Billingham and Redcar. The region is still dominated by its heavy engineering, its steel, oil and chemical industries.

If you imagine, however, that Cleveland is nothing but heavy industry, you couldn't be more wrong. The county contains areas of spectacular countryside, including part of The North York Moors National Park, some superb stretches of coastline, as dramatic as anything in England, and, in the Tees valley itself, towns and villages of great charm and historic interest. Roseberry Topping, a strange conical hill, landmark and view-point, lies exactly on Cleveland's boundary with North Yorkshire and the view from its summit takes in the greater part of this compact but varied lesser known county.

The most famous individual to come from Cleveland was, of course, Captain James Cook, discoverer of much of Australasia. He was born on 27th October 1927, the son of a farm labourer, in a simple cottage at Marton, a village just off the A172 south of Middlesborough. Cook was baptised in the local parish church and educated at the village school. When he was eight, the family moved to Aireyholme Farm, near Great Ayton, where he was later taken on as a farm boy before being sent to Staithes as apprentice to a grocer. But his ambition to see the world proved stronger, and the young man was eventually allowed to become a sailor at the nearby port of Whitby (at that time the centre of the whaling industry) and this led to his distinguished career in the Royal Navy as mariner and explorer without equal.

The Captain Cook Birthplace Museum now stands in the grounds of Stewart Park, Marton, only 40 metres from the actual site of the thatched cottage, now demolished, where he was born. Exhibitions illustrate in an imaginative way many aspects of Cook's life and include a reconstruction of the galley of a Royal Naval vessel as Cook would have known it. The museum forms part of the Cook Heritage Trail, which leads through the many places in Cleveland and North Yorkshire associated with James Cook.

Perhaps Cleveland's greatest claim to fame, though, was as the birthplace of the world's first commercially successful public steam-railway, which ran from Darlington to Stockton and which opened in 1825.

Both **Yarm** and **Stockton** were once busy ports on the Tees, Yarm being the highest point that loaded ships could reach along the increasingly serpentine river before having to unload onto what, in those days, was slow and expensive horse-drawn transport.

It was a group of both Yarm and Stockton businessmen who, as far back as 1810, realised that competition from the new mines and the ports along the Tyne threatened their livelihood. At a celebration dinner in 1810 at Stockton's Town House (Town Hall), Leonard Raisbeck, the town's Recorder, successfully moved a resolution to establish a committee to enquire into the building of a canal or railway to Darlington and the Durham coalfields.

After much argument a railway scheme was chosen, thanks to the visionary backing of the project by Darlington Quaker and banker, Edward Pease. George Stephenson, a relatively unknown Tyneside engine wright, was appointed to oversee its construction. The first sod was cut in May 1822, in what is now Bridge Road, Stockton and, on 27th September 1825, Stephenson's famous engine, 'Locomotion', with a line of coal waggons, made its historic trip into the town.

At the Tourist Information Centre and Museum in the beautifully restored 18th century Green Dragon Yard, you can buy a fascinating 'Stockton Rail Trail' brochure which leads the visitor around the handsome Georgian town, with its High Street - reputedly the broadest in the North of England - past the famous Town House where the idea of the railway was first proposed. The trail leads to Bridge Road where the first sod was cut and where a building still survives that was used to sell tickets. At the riverside, you can still see the remains of the coal staithes where good Durham coal was put into waiting ships for transport down the Tees to London. If you walk across the road bridge from Stockton's twin township of Thornaby-on-Tees, there are good views of this riverside area; and you can follow the Tees Heritage Trail from this point right along the riverside, past the original Stockton rail-terminus, as far as the famous Transporter Bridge in Middlesbrough.

Those who like to explore historic and interesting countryside from a base which provides all the facilities of a large modern hotel will find **The Golden Eagle Hotel** an excellent choice. Situated in **Thornaby on Tees,** this popular and luxurious hotel is within easy reach of the beautiful and striking area known as Captain Cook Country.

The hotel caters for quite contrasting tastes: on the first floor the well patronised Cocktail Bar is elegantly stylish, while the traditional 'olde worlde' theme of one of the ground floor lounges re-creates the atmosphere of a quaint English pub.

Fitness and sporting enthusiasts will be pleased that the hotel had the foresight to become a member of a nearby luxury squash club. Hotel guests can enjoy playing squash here and can also take advantage of the gym facilities. The sauna and solarium are usually preferred by more leisurely guests! Another benefit offered by the hotel is its proximity to a leisure complex where residents of the Golden Eagle are welcome.

Within the hotel itself the Beaufront Restaurant offers a comprehensive menu, with the full a la carte featuring French cuisine. More informal bar meals are served in both lounge bars. Evening entertainment focuses on 'Dynasty's', the hotel's night club.

Despite its size and range of facilities, this is still a family owned hotel where the personal touch is highly valued.

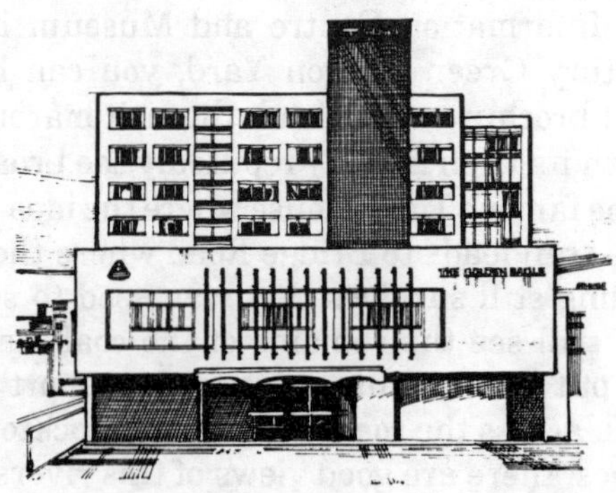

The Golden Eagle Hotel

It is interesting to reflect that the Stockton and Darlington Line was originally planned as a freight railway, and passengers were only carried as an afterthought. It was some time before the first purpose-built stations were constructed; passengers buying their tickets at country inns, as they used to in coaching days, and climbing on board what looked remarkably like a stage-coach from the trackside. Most of the old inns in Stockton which were also ticket offices have long gone, but at Dinsdale, the inn can still be seen, adjacent to the old railway line which is now a disused siding.

Stockton's superb country house and park, Preston Park, on the A135 near Eaglescliffe, actually has part of the original trackbed of The Stockton and Darlington Railway in its grounds. This is probably the site of the famous Terence Cuneo painting of the race which allegedly took place between a passing stage-coach and 'Locomotion' at a point where the road ran parallel to the railway - nobody knows who won.

There is a comforting air about the **Sheraton Hotel** on Yarm Road. While there may be something in the fact that this was once a maternity nursing-home, guests are more likley to agree that the credit really goes to the warm hospitality of Anne and Mike Jenkins.

Sheraton Hotel

In this family-run hotel, the accommodation is comfortable and the atmosphere very informal. Children and pets are welcomed and catered for, as Anne and Mike like their family guests to feel at home. Each of the

16 individually decorated bedrooms has its own character and all have a colour television and tea-making facilities. Other necessary amenities are readily available in the hotel. The decor is traditional to enhance the character of this interesting 19th century building.

Anne enjoys cooking and this is reflected in the breakfast and evening meals, which are home-cooked with fresh produce. The hotel has a residential license, and for the convenience of the guests there is a bar lounge.

Yarm, higher up the Tees on a great bend of the river, has remained a small Georgian town and river port, compared to the transformation of its neighbour, Stockton, by the Industrial Revolution. It remains a town of great charm, with a parish church, hidden beyond the great multi-arched brick railway viaduct, an early Methodist church, handsome town houses, warehouses and shops. There are several fine old coaching inns and, like Stockton, a town hall where the names of Yarm men who supported that remarkable pioneering railway are inscribed on a plaque. There is a lovely riverside walk leading to Yarm's old multi-arched road bridge, which dates back, more or less in its present form, to 1400. You can even make out the difference in size of one of the arches, which once contained a drawbridge which was lifted to allow sailing boats to go through.

Clive and Heather Addison's working farm near Maltby, east of Yarm, is steeped in history and atmosphere. Set on the edge of the North Yorkshire Moors, a few miles off the A19, the accommodation at **Maltby Farm** looks out over the Cleveland Hills.

Maltby Farm

An inscription on the barn doors showing sailing ships and the date 1784 is intriguing; until the history of the building is revealed. This traditional Yorkshire farmhouse, over 200 years old, was reputedly built from Dutch bricks brought back as ballast in empty ships returning from taking wool to Holland. Inside, solid wood doors and low ceilings with their original beams all harmonise to create the feeling of stepping back in time. Stone cheese-presses installed in the garden will arouse further curiosity.

Whether on business or pleasure, guests are warmly welcomed and offered comfortable accommodation, breakfast and evening dinner. There are modern facilities including central heating in the charming, spacious bedrooms, while the old-fashioned lounge has an inviting open fire and, for those who need a reminder of the 20th century, a colour televison.

At **Leven Close Farm**, **High Leven**, Mrs Marjorie Simpson offers a truly friendly welcome to visitors to her comfortable home. Leven Close has three bedrooms (two doubles, one family room) all furnished with antiques: the king-size Victorian beds are a notable example. All the rooms have hand-basins and there is a television lounge for guests not wanting to miss that 'special' programme. Evening meals are provided on request.

Leven Close Farm is a mixed working farm which has cattle, sheep and various crops. It is close to a leisure centre, and facilities for riding and golf are within easy reach.

Middlesbrough, unlike Stockton, actually owes its existence to The Stockton and Darlington Railway, being probably the world's first town built on what had been inhospitable Tees mudflats and developed to serve the needs of the railway. It provided the base for the new Cleveland iron industry which the railway, transporting huge quantities of cheap coal, iron ore and limestone, made possible. Ironically, the growth of Middlesbrough as a great rail-served port, on what had been initially merely a branch of the original Stockton and Darlington Railway, heralded the decline of Stockton as a major port.

The town is a fine example of enlightened Victorian town planning with its grid of handsome streets, and there are many fine buildings, including the Town Hall and Municipal Buildings executed in handsome Gothic style. The Art Gallery, in a huge Victorian house in Linthorpe Road, has one of the most important collections of 20th century British Art in the North-East. Close to the main entrance to Albert Park is the Dorman Museum, whose displays include 'The Making of Modern Middlesbrough' and collections of richly glazed Linthorpe Pottery.

Perhaps Middlesbrough's most famous landmark, however, is the great Transporter Bridge, built in 1911 and of remarkable proportions, being

850ft long and 225ft high, a marvel of Edwardian engineering. It remains in everyday use and carries up to 12 cars and 200 people on each crossing. It rivals Newport Bridge on the Stockton Road, opened in 1834, which also has a claim to engineering fame, being the largest surviving lift-span bridge in the world.

Along Flatts Lane is the **Norman Conquest Hotel**, a modern establishment which has been decorated and furnished in cottage style to a very high standard.

The hotel has eight guest rooms, all with facilities en-suite, and offers comfort and good service to residents and non-residents alike.

Its restaurant seats up to 52 people and provides an excellent choice of dishes and children's menus, all at affordable prices, while the bar serves hot snacks, sandwiches and daily 'specials' at both lunchtime and in the evening. A games room and very spacious lounge all add to the visitor's enjoyment.

The Norman Conquest can accommodate wedding receptions and other private functions up to a capacity of 70 persons.

Norman Conquest Hotel

Immediately south of Middlesbrough lies Ormesby Hall, a fine mid-18th century country house, richly decorated internally with some exceptional plasterwork. There are fine gardens, a courtyard and a lovely stable block attributed to Carr of York. Managed by The National Trust, it has a tea-room and shop. Less than four miles away, near Lazenby village just south of the main A174 Redcar road, is Lazenby Bank, an area of wooded hillside climbing up to Eston Nab, one of the best viewpoints in Cleveland. As well as a car park there are waymarked walks and a number of items of industrial heritage interest, including the line of an old tramway.

The **Southern Cross Hotel** at **Marton** offers comfortable and modern bed and breakfast accommodation, and has the Chandlers Restaurant, popular with residents and non-residents alike for 'memorable, affordable eating out'.

The 'Carvery' is particularly good value, since diners can eat as much as they wish, for a fixed price. There is a selection of seven starters, at least as many desserts and, for the main course, the chef will offer a selection of freshly prepared roasts accompanied by vegetables or salad.

No less tempting is the 'Steak Menu', and again the portions are generous. After starters, which may prove to be meals in themselves, diners may choose a dish prepared with their favourite cut of steak, served with one of the seven special house-sauces. For those with a hearty appetite, there is the choice of prime 2lb rib steak!

Southern Cross Hotel

Redcar, close to **Middlesbrough** and the expansive industry of Teesside, offers a remarkable contrast - a lively and attractive small seaside resort, with all you would expect of a seaside town. There are good sandy beaches, a promenade, lively sea-front entertainment, all the usual facilities and a Lifeboat Museum. **Leo's Pub Club**, on the Esplanade, is especially well-worth visiting and welcomes visitors both young and old.

Leo's Pub Club

At the end of the promenade - at 196 High Street - is the **Claxton Hotel,** a solid red brick building about 100 years old, which gives clear views of the sea.

This hotel has 18 guest rooms, three of which are on the ground floor and are suitable for disabled visitors: the staff are always available to help, if required. The friendly proprietors, Walter and June Brittain, welcome children, and baby-listening services can be arranged on request.

Claxton Hotel

The Claxton Hotel is licensed for residents and their guests and has a pleasant bar (with pool table) which is part of a large 'olde worlde' function room - a striking feature of which is an inglenook fireplace. This room seats up to 120 people and is a very popular venue for wedding receptions, birthday celebrations and anniversary parties. A separate residents' lounge is available and there are also colour televisions in all the bedrooms, together with tea and coffee making facilities.

Places of interest near to the Claxton Hotel include the Kirkleatham Museum with its park, and the Maritime Museum, which houses the oldest lifeboat in the world.

The headquarters of Langbaurgh-on-Tees' Museum Service is housed in **Kirkleatham Old Hall**, an early-18th century building originally built as a free school. It is just one of a number of important historic buildings and features which bear testimony to the wealth and community spirit of the Turner family, and which now form part of an outstanding conservation area.

Kirkleatham village, its church and population, were mentioned in the Norman Domesday survey of 1086. From the 1620s onwards, the Turner family, whose wealth was based on local mining, agriculture, the woollen industry and the law, developed a country estate based around the village, the church and their own residence, Kirkleatham Hall.

Kirkleatham Old Hall Museum

Although the hall itself has disappeared, the large 1720s stable block by James Gibbs, survives alongside various garden features, arches and fortified towers. In the 1740s, Gibbs added the unique mausoleum to the church as a memorial to Marwood Turner, who died in France whilst on the Grand Tour. Today it contains other fine memorials and statues to the Turners.

Sir William Turner, probably the most famous of the family, endowed the Turner Hospital in the 1670s for the housing of 10 poor men, 10 poor women and 20 orphan children. In the 18th century, the hospital was remodelled and a magnificent chapel built by James Gibbs. This contains mahogany stalls, a marble floor, magnificent stained glass and other interesting features. It is still used today as a home for senior citizens.

Kirkleatham Old Hall, opened in 1709 as a free school, housed Yorkshire's second oldest public museum from around 1730 to 1780. Some of its exhibits survive today in other institutions, but the present museum, opened in 1981 in a restored 'Old Hall', now houses collections which are used to tell the story of Langbaurgh past and present and its people. The displays feature geological and archaeological material; natural history specimens; working-life objects reflecting the area's important mining, metalworking and chemical industries; maritime collections; a reconstructed seaside-rock and sweet-making workshop; domestic-life objects; paintings; photographs and a changing programme of lively exhibitions and events. Other visitor attractions include a shop, cafeteria, aviary, gardens and a children's play area and picnic area, all of which make for a great day out.

The museum and its parent body, Langbaurgh-on-Tees Borough Council, also operate or support other museum projects in the area, including the Zetland Museum of Shipping and Fishing in Redcar, which houses the oldest surviving lifeboat in the world, the 'Zetland' (built 1802); the Tom Leonard Mining Museum, Skinningrove and the Guisborough Museum.

There are also other, not so well known, places in this part of Cleveland, which are well worth discovering.

Marske-by-the-Sea is a case in point. This is a quiet, pleasant little seaside town, with a beach where you'll find a scattering of fishermen's boats and the timber-framed Ship Inn. The ruined tower of St Germain's church on the cliff-top is the only remaining part of the building, which was demolished in 1960. Captain Cook's father and sister lie buried in the churchyard, his father dying in 1779, unaware that his son had died six weeks earlier. Nearby Marske Hall, on the other side of the A1085, is also worth a visit.

Marske Hall

South of Marske lies **Errington Wood**, owned by Langbaurgh Borough Council - 200 acres of beautiful woodland, known for its bluebells and other wild flowers, with car parks and over nine miles of waymarked paths.

Further east along the coast is that delightful Victorian seaside resort, **Saltburn,** which once had a railway station inside its imposing **Zetland** Hotel. A remarkable survivor from Victorian times is the rare water-powered funicular railway, which climbs 207ft to the cliff top along which runs the 110 mile Cleveland Way. You can follow part of The Cleveland Way along the cliff top, via **Skinningrove** and **Boulby** to **Staithes**, a walk of about nine miles on some of the highest cliffs in England, most of it lying within the Cleveland Heritage Coast.

At Skinningrove, along the coast between Saltburn and Staithes, you'll find the Tom Leonard Mining Museum, a restored group of buildings which include 'Engine House' and 'Fan House', part of a drift mine, and a collection of tools and artifacts, photographs and memorabilia which once formed part of the Cleveland ironstone industry.

Nearby Loftus Woods has a choice of walks, down a series of wooded valleys, including a lovely beckside walk, past Loftus Dam.

Highcliffe Cottage, blessed with glorious views, is an ideal base from which to explore the surrounding countryside and coastal area of National Park and Heritage status. The charming, stone, self-catering cottage is part of Street House Farm, near Loftus, which has been with the same family since 1830. Betty Garbutt, presently in partnership with Simon Jones, is the fifth generation to live at the farm.

Highcliffe Cottage

Visitors are gladly shown around the 250-acre working farm, which also stocks rare breeds of pigs, Leicester Longwood sheep and horses. Pony-and-trap lessons and rides can be arranged: Betty's equestrian skills are internationally renowned.

The farm is popular with naturalists, particularly birdwatchers, and part of it has been designated a Site of Special Scientific Interest - for within its boundaries are the sites of four ancient settlements spanning several historical periods.

Well known breeders of pedigree stock and seasoned winners of championships, the partners offer weekend courses in sheep management, designed to give a thorough grounding in show preparation. And for those who are able to spin and would now like to learn to colour their yarn, Betty also offers an introductory course in rainbow dyeing.

Many of the villages in this area reveal their links with the former ironstone industry. From **Brotton** there are particularly lovely views across the East Cleveland countryside, but two of the most attractive villages are **Easington** and **Moorsholm,** the latter with a Norman-style Victorian church. A little further inland is a town not to be missed - Guisborough - which was, in fact, the ancient capital of the region in Anglo-Saxon times. Things to see include the remains of the 12th century Augustinian Priory (once a rich and powerful foundation), the 15th century Priory Church and the market square with its 18th century cross. The market, established over 600 years ago, takes place on Thursdays and Saturdays. Superb woodlands - Guisborough Woods - slope up above the town into the National Park, and footpaths climb through the woods onto the wide open spaces of Guisborough Moor.

Castle Eden Walkway Visitor Centre

North of the Tees, the countryside is less dramatic, but there is still much to see. Especially popular is the **Castle Eden Walkway Country Park,** which follows a branch route of a once busy railway line which enjoyed 91 years of active service until its final demise in the late 1960s. Left almost undisturbed during nearly 10 years after the track, ballast and other equipment were removed, the area was to become a linear haven for wildlife. Part of this area was acquired by Cleveland County Council, and in 1981 it was properly opened for public recreation.

The old station-house is now a Visitor Centre and shop with some fascinating displays of railway artifacts and local wildlife. From here, footpaths lead to the old track and grassy embankments, now home to the largest variety of butterflies in Cleveland. Nearby Thorpe Wood Local Nature Reserve is carpeted in spring with bluebells and wood anemonies, and a large pond provides a wildlife focus. There are waymarked trails, picnic and adventure play areas, organised special events and an excellent warden service to provide information or assistance.

Greatham, between Billingham and Hartlepool, is a village of some charm and historic interest where, every Boxing Day, the Greatham Sword Dance is performed outside the church gates. This is an area noted for birdlife, and ornithologists come to see a variety of wildfowl on the nearby Cowpen Marshes. North Gare and South Gare, with its sand dunes and breakwater, on the other side of the Tees, are also popular with birdwatchers as well as for viewing the Teesside shipping.

Hartlepool dates back to medieval times. It was once a walled town and port, the remains of whose walls can still be seen on the south side of the headland, as can the impressive 12th century church of St Hilda. An old tale tells of how, in Hartlepool, during Napoleonic times, a monkey dressed in military uniform was reputedly washed ashore on a raft and, gibbering with fright, was believed by local people to be speaking French. It was publicly hanged as a spy!

There is an exceptionally interesting Maritime Museum, which traces the growth of the town from Saxon and Viking times to the development of the Victorian dock and shipbuilding complexes. Among the displays are an early gas-lit lighthouse lantern and a reconstructed fisherman's cottage. You can also see HMS 'Warrior', Britain's first iron-clad battleship, being restored by the Ships Preservation Trust. Gray Art Gallery and Museum, in a mid-Victorian mansion in Clarence Road, with its fine collection of paintings and extensive displays of archaeology, should not be missed. The town itself has a large, covered market and modern shopping centre.

The Grand Hotel, on Swainson Street, prides itself on being able to claim that its guests have been returning time and again. An impression of being somewhere special is created immediately on entering the spacious and tastefully renovated entrance hall of this Grade II listed building, where the staff will extend a warm and friendly welcome. Both businessmen and holidaymakers will find the hotel convenient for the A19 and A1(M), local railway services and Teesside Airport.

The well-equipped bedrooms are large and elegant and most are en-suite. There are facilities for disabled guests, including a passenger lift serving all floors.

On the ground floor, Victoria's Lounge Bar offers an extensive selection of drinks and a varied bar menu at lunchtime. Alternatively, there is the Piper's Restaurant, renowned for its Carvery and a la carte menus, where a more substantial lunch or dinner may be enjoyed along with some fine wines.

Energetic guests may choose to enjoy some time at the sound-proofed Images Disco Bar, situated on the lower ground floor. Other facilities include the magnificent Victorian Ballroom, a number of private rooms and an inter-communicating suite for social functions and business meetings.

The Grand Hotel

Like Middlesbrough, Hartlepool has a pleasant rural hinterland, with some charming and ancient villages. Hart, for instance, from which Hartlepool gets its name, reputedly the birthplace of Robert the Bruce; Elwick, noted for its wide village greens and cosy pubs; and Dalton Piercy, from where there are long views across the town to Hartlepool Bay.

Pease's House, Darlington

Central Durham

Lumley Castle

CHAPTER TWO

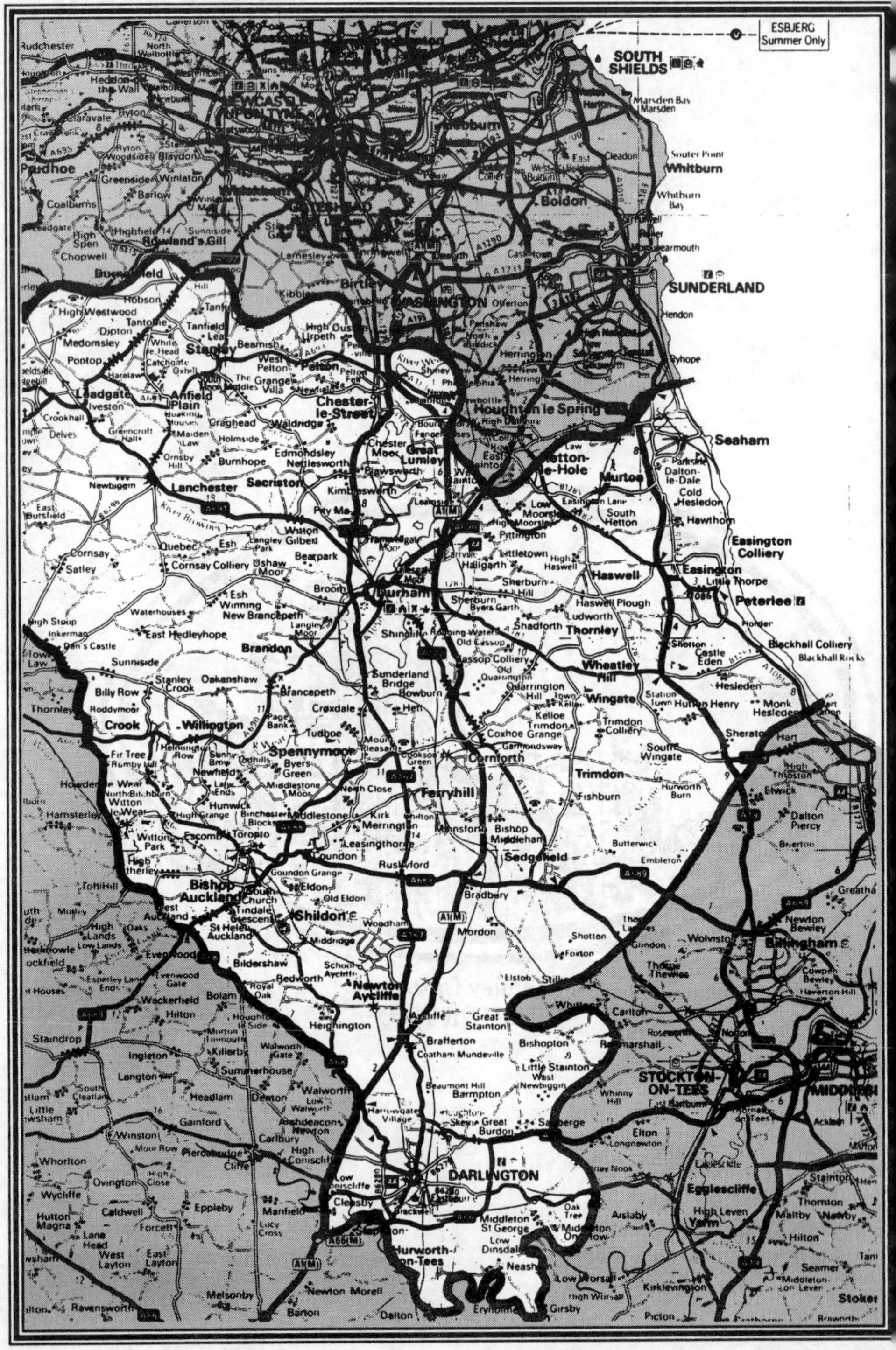

Chapter Two - Map Reference Guide
Central Durham

Mount Pleasant Hotel - Consett

Bernhardt Gallery - Darlington

Uplands Hotel - Crook

Walworth Castle Hotel - Walworth

'Adolphus' - Seaham

Crombies Restaurant & Guest House - Darlington

Crown & Crossed Swords - Shotley Bridge

Leap Mill Farm - Burnopfield

Dunvegan Guest House - Durham

Waldridge Hall Farm - Old Waldridge

Castledene - Durham

Old Manor House Hotel - West Auckland

Bygones Antiques - Darlington

The Hat & Feather - Medomsley

Pondfield Villa - Rowley

Oak Tree Inn - Tantobie

Park Head Hotel - New Coundon

Tanfield Railway - Stanley

Tynemouth

CHAPTER TWO

Central Durham

If you arrive in **Durham** by train, as you approach the station across the elevated brick viaduct above the town, there is a magnificent view of Durham city, dominated by its mighty cathedral.

No visit to Durham is complete without time spent at this magnificent shrine of Christianity, third only to Canterbury and York in ecclesiastical significance but perhaps even excelling them in architectural splendour. It is acknowledged to be the finest and grandest example of early Norman architecture in the kingdom.

This was the cathedral of the powerful and wealthy Prince Bishops of Durham who once held almost regal power in their territories - power vested in them by King William II. They could administer civil and criminal law; they had the power of pardon and the right to mint their own money, create baronetcies, and give market charters; they could even raise their own army! It is little wonder that the County Council now proudly present their county to visitors as 'The Land of the Prince Bishops'.

Even more significantly, in the great cathedral are the tombs of two of the greatest figures of the early Christian church in England: the remarkable St Cuthbert, shepherd saint of Northumbria, and the Venerable Bede, saint and scholar, Britain's first and pre-eminent historian.

The cathedral owes its origin to a Saxon Benedictine community who, in 995AD, fled to this rocky peninsula which is surrounded by the serpentine River Wear, to hide the body of their beloved St Cuthbert in a little church made from the boughs of trees.

The real founder of the cathedral, however, was a Norman, William de St Carileph, the Bishop of Durham from 1081 to 1096, who brought to the small Saxon church at Durham not only holy relics but also a group of scholars from Monkwearmouth and Jarrow.

William was exiled to Normandy in 1088, having been accused of plotting against William Rufus, but returned in 1091 determined to replace the little Saxon church with a building of the scale and style of the splendid new churches being built in France at that time. On 10th August 1093 the foundation stones were laid, a witness being King Malcom III of Scotland, famed as the soldier who conquered and slew Macbeth.

The main part of the great building was erected in a mere 40 years, but over ensuing centuries each generation has added magnificent work or superb detail of its own, such as the Episcopal Throne, said to be the highest in Christendom. Yet the impregnable fortress-like quality of the cathedral, with its famous carved columns, has kept an architectural unity and visual splendour that makes it a very special place indeed. Even so, nothing is more moving than the simple fragments of carved wood which survive from St Cuthbert's coffin, made for the saint's body in 698AD and carried around a hostile North of England for almost 300 years by his devoted followers before being laid to rest in the mighty cathedral. The fragments are now kept in the Cathedral Treasury Museum with examples of the Prince Bishops' own silver coins.

The pump at College Green, Durham City

Durham Castle, sharing the same rocky peninsula and standing close to the cathedral, was founded in 1072 and belonged to the Prince Bishops. Such was the impregnability of the site that Durham was one of the few major towns in Northumbria that was never captured by the Scots.

Amongst its most impressive features are the Chapel, dating from 1080, and the Great Hall, which was built in the middle of the 13th century. Though much of the building was restored in Victorian times, it remains a remarkable building in its own right.

The city itself reflects the long history of the castle and cathedral it served, including generations of pilgrims who had to be fed and watered - arguably Britain's first tourists! There are winding streets, such as Fishergate and Silver Street, whose names and appearance reveal their medieval origin, an ancient Market Place, elegant Georgian houses, particularly around Palace Green, quiet courts and alleyways. Yet, for all its industrial development in the 19th and 20th centuries, there is a sense of green-ness and open space, never more evident than in the view across the town from the University or in the fine park behind the railway station.

Those looking for conveniently situated accommodation will find the attractive Edwardian terraced house, **Castledene,** in Nevilledale Terrace. It is certainly well placed for touring Durham City and is in easy walking distance of the many places of interest the city has to offer. Your hostess, Mrs Byrne, will make you very welcome and you will find that the spacious accommodation is not only comfortable and warm with full central heating, but absolutely spotless throughout. There are two twin bedrooms and one single room available, all with tea and coffee making facilities. The twin rooms also benefit from colour television. There is ample private parking available and after a tiring day spent exploring the city, you can relax in comfort in the guests' lounge before you retire to bed.

Castledene

Dunvegan Guest House is owned by Mrs Alma Roach who, as Secretary of the Durham City Guest House Association, will ensure that your stay is extremely comfortable! Because of her links with the City, Mrs Roach can give visitors a first-hand account of what to see and do in Durham and the immediate locale. Situated on the A167 heading out of Durham towards Darlington, the house stands in beautifully tended gardens of half an acre. Each room including en-suite is impeccably furnished, with tea and coffee making facilities and colour television provided. A full English breakfast will get you off to a good start for the day, and a wide range of bar meals can be enjoyed at the inn that is situated close by. With attractions like the Beamish Museum and the Metro Centre nearby and the lovely Durham Dales for touring, this is an excellent holiday base. Dunvegan has been awarded a Two Crown English Tourist Board classification, so you know you are dealing with a professional who knows how to look after her guests.

Dunvegan Guest House

A favourite and famous walk past castle and cathedral follows the footpaths which run through the woodlands on each bank of the River Wear, around the great loop. You can begin either at Framwellgate Bridge or Elvet Bridge. The path along the outside of the loop goes past The Old Fulling Mill, which now houses an archaeological museum containing material from excavations in and around the city. If walking isn't to your taste you can take a rowing-boat or a motor launch along the river from Elvet Bridge.

A very different museum but outstanding in a quite different way, is the

Durham University Oriental Museum, a collection of oriental art of international importance with material from Ancient Egypt, Tibet, India and China. The university also runs the 18-acre Botanic Gardens on Hollingworth Lane (off the A1050).

If, on the other hand, you want to discover a lovely piece of Durham away from the main tourist trails, make your way by car or bus to Finchale Priory, still on the River Wear, some four miles north of the city, on the Leamside-Newton Hall road. This is a 13th century Benedictine Priory which, amazingly enough, was actually built as a holiday retreat for the monks of Durham. There are extensive remains and they lie close to Cocken Wood Picnic Area, which is linked to the priory by a bridge across the river.

It's not a long journey from Durham to Beamish Open Air Museum, some five miles north-west of Chester-le-Street, an award-winning museum situated in 200 acres of landscaped parkland in which life in County Durham a century or so ago has been vividly re-created. There is a tramway serving old mining communities; a drift mine; streets with cottages, shops and a pub; there is also a railway and a working farm.

More industrial heritage is to be found nearby at Causey Arch, the oldest surviving railway bridge in the world. Dating from 1725, it crosses an 80ft wooded gorge carrying an early waggonway to and from nearby collieries. It can be reached along the A6076 Gateshead road. There is a picnic site nearby with an interpretive display explaining the history of this remarkable structure.

Causey Arch

The **Tanfield Railway**, which runs between Marley Hill, near Stanley, and Sunniside, is the oldest existing railway in the world, being a colliery waggonway (not a public railway) dating from 1725. It is now a private steam railway with a collection of vintage locomotives, carriages and Britain's oldest steam engine shed which dates back to 1855. There is a Sunday passenger service (steam-worked in summer) and an extension to Causey Arch picnic area was completed in summer 1990.

Lanchester, some seven miles north-west of Durham, owes its name to the Roman fort of Longovicium, the foundations of which survive on a hilltop half a mile to the west. The fort was built to guard Dere Street, the Roman road which linked Hadrian's Wall and York. Stone from the fort was used in the Norman Church of All Saints, and Roman pillars can be seen supporting the north aisle; there is a Roman altar in the south porch and three beautiful pieces of 13th century stained glass in the south window.

In **Consett**, visitors will find comfortable accommodation in 10 family rooms at **The Mount Pleasant Hotel,** which is run by Neil Campbell.

The hotel has something of a split personality: the character of the bar reflects the age of the old part of the building and, appropriately, serves traditional Real Ale. In contrast, the main part of the hotel houses a modern function room called Lacey's where there are discos, dancing and wedding parties.

Open all the year round, this is in easy reach of the picturesque Vale of Derwent, and various reservoirs provide additional scenic views. Pony trekking is one of the activities popular in the area, and Beamish Museum is near enough for a most enjoyable day's visit. Newcomers to this area also like to visit the Gateshead Metro Centre, one of the largest shopping centres in Europe.

Mount Pleasant Hotel

Rowley lies to the south of Consett on the A68. **Pondfield Villa,** just a short way from the village, has to be one of the best guesthouses around - for one very important reason. They cater especially for those with disabilities, and it is obvious that a great deal of thought has gone into the design of the building. Keith Watson is a former motorbike racer, who saw many colleagues suffering injuries that left them disabled. With this in mind he got together with Valerie Beck, a local girl who is disabled, and with her advice to guide him put together a first class bed and breakfast accommodation unit and activity centre.

The rooms benefit from larger doors, sit down showers, emergency cords in every room and a spaciousness which those in wheelchairs will particularly appreciate. Pond Villa also welcomes the able bodied, of course, and by the time we go to press, more rooms should be available for them. The main block has five rooms and there is an eight-berth static caravan site, as well as a 5,000 sq ft greenhouse/market garden with cafe, quad bikes and even pony rides. The 20-acre site has been designed to provide fun for all ages and Keith and his wife Eileen have many plans for further developments. We wish them well for the future. To find them, take the A68 heading south, turn left past Rowley and head towards Lanchester. Take the first right and Pondfield Villa is a short way down the road on your left.

Pondfield Villa

Steel making first started in this area at Shotley Bridge, when craftsmen from Germany set up their furnaces in the 17th century and began making swords. Now a smart northern suburb of Consett, it is hard to believe that it was still a steelmaking town as recently as 1983. When the railway came here to serve the local iron works and surrounding collieries in the 19th century, Shotley Bridge began to develop something of a reputation as a spa town, and its popularity as such is evident from the many grand houses to be seen here. Although the railway closed down many years ago, the line has now been transformed into a scenic walkway, and it is possible to walk or cycle along the 10-mile route following the valley downhill to Swalwell.

The **Crown and Crossed Swords** has been in Sheila Suddick's family for around 43 years. Sheila, together with husband Cy, took over from her parents five years ago and they have successfully upheld the high reputation that the inn is renowned for. This traditional inn can be found in the heart of Shotley Bridge, and as a former coaching house, the mail coaches would have passed through here on their way to Northumberland and Scotland. In the car park, the livery stables can still be seen. In addition to the tasty bar meals on offer, good, traditional English food is served in the restaurant in the evenings, and on Sundays a full roast lunch can be enjoyed. It is well worth booking for this, as Sunday's offering always proves popular with the locals! There are 10 rooms available at the inn for bed and breakfast, five of them en-suite, and the accommodation is very good value for money.

The Crown and Crossed Swords

Just to the north-east on the B6310 is the village of **Medomsley,** where we came across the oddly named pub, **The Hat & Feather**. Owners Danny and Micheal Hodkinson were intrigued to know where the name came from, as they believe it to be the only pub in England with that name. It has always been called The Hat & Feather and was most probably an old coaching house.

We had heard of a 'Hat and Beaver' in Atherstone, Warwickshire, where hatmaking was quite an established industry. However, the name 'Feathers' is said to hark back to 1346 when the Black Prince, son of Edward III, won the battle of Crecy. He reputedly took the ostrich feather crest that had been the standard of John of Bohemia and claimed the symbol and motto 'Ich dien' for his own coat of arms. Since then, the 'Feathers' has been adopted as the crest for every succeeding Prince of Wales, down to our present Prince Charles. If you see 'Feathers' on its own, it usually means that the locals or the innkeeper were loyal to the Prince of Wales of their era. What is so fitting is that the German motto means 'I serve', so it could not be more apt!

The Hat & Feather also has a resident ghost, although the Hodkinsons have yet to catch a glimpse of him or her. It always surprises us how few pubs own up to having a ghost, as in our experince it usually brings people flocking!.

The Hat & Feather

Micheal trained as a chef and so the restaurant benefits from an excellent a la carte menu, with such evocative dishes as 'Trout in Pernod sauce' earning it a fine local reputation. The bar offers all the benefits of a traditional village pub and it is very popular with the locals. We found the pub to be very welcoming, the sort of place where you can linger over a meal and a drink without anyone hurrying you along. Danny and Micheal both take a keen interest in local history, and around the walls are many old photographs of the area relating to its mining and iron working past. They are still waiting to get a snapshot of that ghost, and we wish them the best of luck!

Further along the road at Burnopfield, we had an opportunity to look at a wonderful restored 18th century water mill at **Leap Mill Farm.** Owners Mary and Ronald Barrass have cherished their dream of restoring the mill for the past 30 years, and at last they have succeeded. In addition to the mill, you can also enjoy Mary's farmhouse teas while relaxing in the sunken garden and admiring the rare farm breeds which roam about the farm. The water wheel is said to be unique in County Durham, so be sure to make this one of your stopping places if you want to view this very special glimpse of the past

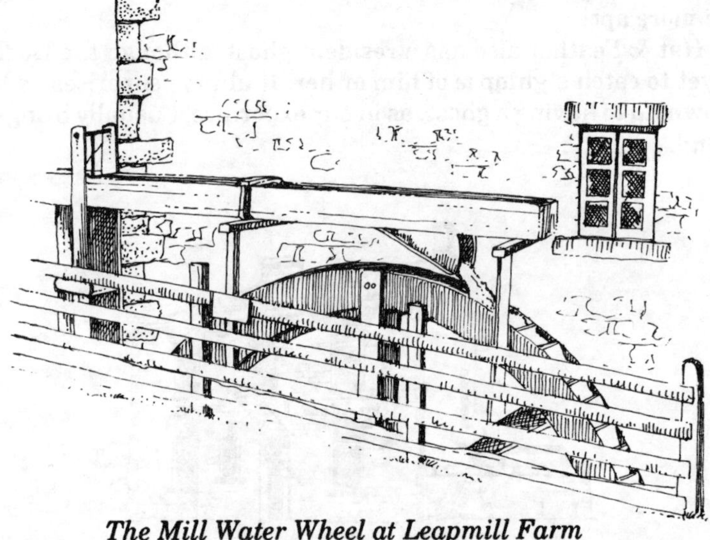

The Mill Water Wheel at Leapmill Farm

The quaintly named village of **Tantobie** lies south-east of here on the B6173, and here we found the **Oak Tree Inn**, run by Sylvia Hurst and her daughter Mandy. Sylvia was born in France, so the cuisine reflects her taste in food and has a real French farmhouse appeal to it. Only fresh produce is used and like all good chefs, she prefers not to hurry her food along while it is cooking. Dishes such as Game Pie and Venison in Ruby Port sound wonderful, but for a real feel of France, you must try the house speciality, 'Choucroute garni', which is the National Dish of Alsace Lorraine. As well as being quite delicious, the meals are also very reasonably priced.

The pretty restaurant with its Victorian lace tablecloths is enchanting, while the decor throughout the Inn is most attractive. Sylvia studied and worked as a designer, and the Oak Tree is a wonderful setting for her flair and creativity. We thought the dining room would make a perfect place for a wedding reception, while on a summer's day, guests can enjoy a barbeque outside in the garden.

Apart from the guest rooms in the main building, the Coach House next door has been converted into three very smart units for overnight letting, and upstairs is a self-contained suite which is superbly appointed. All in all, this is a marvellous place to eat and rest, and all that remains to be said is 'Bon appetit!'

Oak Tree Inn

Chester-le-Street, as its name implies, also owes its existence to a small Roman camp, this time on the main Roman road to Newcastle. It was here that the monks of Lindisfarne laid the body of their beloved St Cuthbert to rest for 113 years in a wooden church. This might have become a great cathedral had not the monks, in 995AD, increasingly threatened by Viking raids, decided to move their precious relic to the safety of the rock on the Wear, to what is now Durham Cathedral.

Of particular interest in Chester-le-Street is the Anker's House Museum, giving unique insight into the Order of Ankerites who were literally walled up in their cells to spend their life in prayer and contemplation. The museum explains the life of an Ankerite or Ankeress with exhibits, history and artifacts of a church which was established in 883AD and continues to the present day.

Waldridge Fell Country Park, two miles south-west of Chester-le-Street, close to **Waldridge** village, is County Durham's last surviving area of lowland heathland, and a car park and waymarked walks give access to over 300 acres of open countryside, rich in natural history interest.

The elegant **Waldridge Hall Farm,** with neatly gravelled drive, ornate railings on the upper windows and supporting portico columns at the front entrance, is the setting for bed and breakfast accommodation in Old Waldridge. Despite its stylish appearance, the welcome you receive is warm and friendly, for this is a family home. Joan and Arthur Smith offer their guests a comfortable and relaxing retreat, and at breakfast you will be rewarded by Joan's homemade preserves and marmalades, made to her own secret recipe! We are pretty sure that after sampling these you will wish to purchase a few pots as a reminder of your stay. Children are always welcome here, which is a sure sign that your hosts are both obliging and friendly. The accommodation consists of one family room and two doubles, and guests have full use of the lounge. With Waldridge Fell within easy walking distance and Beamish and Durham city just a few miles away, this is an ideal base for touring.

Waldridge Hall Farm

At the opposite end of the county, the imposing **Walworth Castle Hotel** lies three miles north-west of the market town of **Darlington**. In its tranquil 18-acre setting of lawns and woods, it is hard to remember that the

A1(M) is but a couple of miles away.

As one might imagine, this 800-year-old castle has had a chequered history before becoming the elegant hotel it is today. Peter and Anita Culley can tell you a great deal about the Castle's past from its origins in 1189, whilst exploring its structural features and interior decorations will put the changing story into persepective: arrow slits visible in the south-west tower date back to the 12th century; in the quadrangle there is a fine Elizabethan porch; and in the East Wing the bay windows are Tudor. Some of the interior plasterwork is Georgian, originating from when General Aylmer owned the castle, and the Aylmer coat-of-arms remains a feature of the striking stained-glass Venetian window on the grand staircase in the North Wing.

Walworth Castle Hotel

Guests, past and present, have been no less interesting, and best noted is the visit of King James VI of Scotland who stayed at the castle in 1603 in what is now the lounge of the King James Suite. Today's visitors include the famous of our time - actors, authors and politicians.

While retaining much of the past grandeur and atmosphere with period furniture and handsome interior decoration, the hotel has been converted luxuriously to provide the comforts of modern amenities. Most bedrooms are en-suite and the doubles have four-poster beds.

Two restaurants offer English and French menus: the 'Hansard' is popular with both residents and non-residents for its excellent cuisine. In the three bars the atmosphere is informal and light meals are available - it is hard to resist the roaring log fire in the 'Farmers' Bar when the cold sets in!

Peter and Anita also cater for conferences and private parties from 120 to small numbers - the Library Turrett lends itself to special exclusiveness.

A unique place to stay accompanied by a very warm welcome, Walworth Castle is ideally situated for several nearby attractions and is accessible for fishing, golfing and walking in the area.

Darlington, just off the Great North Road, has every right to be considered Durham's second town, both in terms of its importance as a regional centre serving the southern part of County Durham and for its heritage - the Railway Age.

It has a bustling town centre, with a large Market Place and grand Victorian Market Hall that bring people in from the surrounding Dales of both Durham and Yorkshire - Market Day is both Monday and Saturday. High Row, with its elevated street of shops, makes an impressive sight and it forms part of a compact but characterful shopping centre. St Cuthbert's Church is a particularly fine example of early English Gothic architecture. The Edwardian Civic Theatre also enjoys an excellent reputation, and there is an impressive museum, with much material from Teesdale as well as Darlington itself, in Tubwell Row.

Crombies Restaurant and Guest House

It was also here that we found **Crombies Restaurant and Guest House,** run by Christina McCallum and her daughter and son-in-law, Maureen and Fredrick Stehr. It is located opposite the Cornmill Shopping Centre in Tubwell Row. Crombies has been run as a family business for three generations, and their relaxing and homely service means that visitors return again and again. Their food has an excellent reputation, with many lunchtime specials being available. In addition to discovering the delights of the menu and enjoying the relaxing atmosphere, you could well find yourself rubbing shoulders with a theatrical celebrity here, as many of these frequent the restaurant on a regular basis. Christina can show you an autograph book that will amaze you. The accommodation offered in this unique establishment is first class, with three single rooms and five doubles available, together with a substantial breakfast which will well and truly set you up to go exploring the lovely towns and villages nearby.

The **Bernhardt Gallery** in Coniscliffe Road is dedicated to the works of local artists. The Gallery has been established for about 13 years and exhibits primarily water colours and etchings, and also offers a picture framing service. Customers come from a very wide area; not only for good service but for something different and original.

Bernhardt Gallery

Mrs Margaret Reynolds took over the Gallery nearly five years ago. Her main aim was to cater for a growing market of original work by local artists. The artists' work shown in the Gallery now covers a wide area of the North, and some comes from as far afield as Norfolk. Margaret worked with her husband in a graphic design consultancy for a few years before making the break on her own. She has exhibitions twice a year, sometimes 'one-man' shows, others mixed.

Margaret also sells limited edition prints and is particularly proud of those by Alan Hunt, who has a considerable reputation locally and is meeting with great approval in America.

As well as seeking out the local art galleries, we always find it great fun to go browsing for antiques and curios - and in McMullen Road we were lucky enough to stumble upon **Bygones Antiques,** which specialises in Victorian and Edwardian furniture. Mike Pitman and his partner Angie Walton have been here for five years and have built up a fine reputation, with clients coming from as far afield as London and Holland. Old farming tools and equipment is always popular with buyers, but customers today are especially on the look-out for domestic artifacts like kitchen ware, tables and fireplaces. You can pick up some fascinating photographs, old glass bottles, church pews, and a huge and diverse range of items to add to your collections.

Bygones Antiques

Mike is also a specialist in cleaning old furniture, using slivers of glass

- definitely not to be tried at home! A four inch sliver (the greenhouse variety is best!) is used to scrape away the old stained wood and reveal the fresh under-layer. Although most furniture renovators strip the wood in chemical baths, Mike insists that his way is kinder to the wood, as it does not destroy the natural oils. As a result, his wooden pieces are truly beautiful. The telephone number for Bygones Antiques is (0325) 461399/ 380884, and business hours are as follows: Monday to Thursday 10.30am - 5.30pm; Friday 10.30am - 4pm; Saturday closed; Sunday viewing 12am - 5pm.

Perhaps Darlington's greatest claim to fame lies in the role the town played with its neighbour, Stockton, in the creation of the world's first commercially successful public railway, The Stockton and Darlington Railway, opened in 1825. It was the Darlington Quaker and Banker, Edward Pease, who became the main driving force behind the railway scheme to link the Durham coalfield with the port of Stockton.

The present Darlington Station at Bank Top came from a much later period in the railway age, as lines were being constructed to link England and Scotland. The original Darlington Station, built in 1842, was at what is now North Road. Today it is the Darlington Railway Centre and Museum, a museum of national importance, housing as it does relics of the pioneering Stockton and Darlington Railway, including Stephenson's 'Locomotion No 1' itself, an early S&D carriage and Hackworth's mighty engine, the 'Derwent'. Timothy Hackworth (1786-1850) came from nearby Shildon and, as Stephenson's Locomotive Superintendent, was the man with the practical skills to make the engines actually work. He designed his own breed of rugged, tough colliery engines, which really demonstrated the superiority of steam power over the horse in terms of strength and reliability. Hackworth also built the first locomotives to be used in Russia (1836) and Canada (1838).

The locomotive works at Shildon have long closed but the Soho Engine Shed and nearby cottage, where Hackworth lived and worked, have been preserved as The Timothy Hackworth Museum. Only a short walk from Shildon Station, the museum can be reached by car from the Bishop Auckland road, via Soho Street and Beverley Road. A replica of Hackworth's locomotive, 'Sans Pareil', can also be found there.

So much early railway history is to be seen in this part of County Durham that British Rail have named their local Bishop Auckland-Darlington-Middlesbrough line, The Heritage Line. Trains on the Bishop Auckland line call at North Road Station, making a visit to the museum particularly convenient by train.

Bishop Auckland lies at the end of the line, except for Sundays during the summer months when trains take visitors on into Weardale as far as Stanhope. Like many similar towns in central Durham, it is a former mining town, slowly discovering a new identity as the new industry replaces the old - but its origins are far older than mining. As its name implies, up until the first part of the 19th century, this was part of the territory of the great Durham Prince Bishops, who controlled what was then a scattering of small villages in the area. Rapid expansion occurred during the 19th century and Bishop Auckland became an important market and administrative centre for the mining region.

Auckland Castle, still the official residence of the Bishop of Durham, began as a small Norman Manor House but was added to by successive Bishops. The ruins of the 12th century Banqueting Hall were transformed into a magnificent Private Chapel in 1665. The castle and extensive grounds, which include a Gothic deer shelter, are open to the public.

The Park Head Hotel is situated in open countryside and can be located half a mile north-east of Bishop Auckland on the A688.

Conveniently close to historical centres such as Durham, Barnards Castle, The Dales and the Beamish Museum, the Hotel is a popular choice of location for tourists who are exploring the area. Sport loving guests benefit too, as the River Wear is ideal for fishing for trout and salmon. Golf fans will be delighted to find Auckland Golf Course within easy walking distance and tennis, squash, bowls, swimming and a health centre are all nearby. If you are really adventurous, remember to have a day out learning to ski at the Willington Leisure Centre.

In 1978 the Hotel underwent intense renovation, from a derelict public house dating back to the 1890s, into a 15-bedroom hotel, with a traditional lounge bar, a 60-seater restaurant and a 180-seater carvery/function room. A further 20 bedrooms and two executive suites were added during 1990.

The bedrooms are all en-suite and tastefully furnished, with colour TV, tea and coffee making facilities, hair dryers and direct dial telephones.

Traditional meals prepared from fresh local produce can be enjoyed in the restaurant, and the chef is always willing to cater for your individual requests.

Adjoining the restaurant and spacious carvery/function room is the lounge bar, a popular meeting place for the guests. The bar is comfortably furnished to enable you to relax with a bar meal or a drink beside the roaring log fire.

The Hotel is particularly popular with the business community, as it offers relaxed conference surroundings close to all the major business centres such as Darlington, Newcastle, Teesside and Sunderland, all on an excellent nearby motorway link. The Hotel's conference room can accommodate up to 150, but smaller rooms are available for select board meetings. Overhead projectors, flip charts and public address systems are provided, and TV and video facilities are available on request.

Park Head Hotel also caters for special occasions. Wedding receptions are supplied with a complimentary bed and breakfast for the bride and groom.

The carvery/function room holds regular discos, cabarets and dances. Their evenings are another attraction at Park Head, with Valentine's Night, Italian, Seafood and French Evenings all providing a four course meal, reasonably priced, and a disco. Private parties and functions are catered for, and all ages are welcome. Their special weekend offer allows customers dining on Friday, Saturday and Sunday night to stay in the comfort of the Hotel's bedrooms at greatly reduced prices.

This is a hotel that certainly has something for everyone; whether your visit is for business or pleasure you are guaranteed to find the Park Head Hotel's facilities exceptional.

Park Head Hotel

A wealth of historic buildings can be found in the surrounding communities of South Church, St Helen Auckland, St Andrew Auckland and West Auckland.

The Old Manor House in **West Auckland** is steeped in history and has close associations with the family of one of our greatest statesmen and prime ministers, Anthony Eden. He was born here in 1897, and his family harks back to the middle of the 15th century when Sir Robert Eden brought his bride Elizabeth Hutton to the Manor. The Manor was built on foundations that date back to the 12th century, and during the 13th century a brewery stood on the site. It passed through Parliamentarian hands in the 16th century and in 1643, John Eden mustered support to aid Charles I. As a direct result of this display of loyalty, his son Robert Eden had the title of Baronet of Auckland bestowed on him by Charles II. In the 'White Room', the beautifully carved images of several members of the Eden family can be seen. Elfrida, Robert, George, Blanche, Caroline and Rose fell victim to the bubonic plague while they were only children, and their carved faces are a touching memorial to the family.

The sumptuous furnishings and decor to be found throughout the house give it a truly regal air, and yet the Old Manor has a genuinely welcoming atmosphere which is enjoyed by both the touring visitor and those who come to take advantage of the superb business and conference facilities provided here.

Some of the finest cuisine in England is served in the charming 'Four Seasons' restaurant, and the chef will be more than happy to cater to your specific requirements. The lounge is exquisitely furnished and decorated, and makes an ideal place to relax in comfort after your meal.

In the 30 en-suite bedrooms you will find colour television, radio, telephone, hairdryer, trouser press and tea and coffee making facilities; providing you with all the modern conveniences whilst still retaining the best of old world style. Four poster bedrooms are also available for that special romantic occasion.

Perhaps the most impressive room of all is the spectacular galleried 'Knights Hall', which is an ideal venue for formal banquets and wedding receptions. Full of character with its original beams and oak panelling, the Hall has a grand, 'baronial' atmosphere and can comfortably seat up to 150 people.

If you enjoy active pursuits you can avail yourself of the excellent leisure centre with its swimming pool, jacuzzi, sauna, solarium and multi-gym. However, if you prefer more sedate ways of relaxing you can take a stroll in the grounds, admiring the flowers and shrubs and the pleasant views of the house.

The Old Manor House really does have something for everyone, and whether you are travelling on business or for pleasure, you will find the staff efficient and friendly and ready to help you get the most out of your stay at this very special hotel.

Old Manor House Hotel

Just one mile walk or drive from Bishop Auckland, along a quiet lane, is Binchester Roman Fort, where the house of the military commander and the best military bath suite (hypocaust) in Britain has survived. Many of the finds from this site are now kept in The Bowes Museum.

As at Lanchester, some of the stones from this fort found their way, probably by barge or raft, up the River Tees to the village of Escomb, about two miles west of Bishop Auckland. Here there is an outstandingly interesting Anglo-Saxon church, claimed by some people to be one of the finest small buildings of its period in Western Europe. Stones from the fort were used in its walls.

Both **Willington** and **Crook** provide a useful base from which to explore this part of lower Weardale. The nine-and-a-half mile Brandon-Bishop Auckland Railway Walk, along a converted railway track, goes through Willington itself and provides a delightful level walk, rich in historic and natural history interest. It goes close by Brancepeth Castle, a medieval baronial castle restored in the 19th century by a Sunderland banker.

Brancepeth is a sheer delight and should not be missed. Most of the original buildings were cleared to make way for Matthew Russell's 're-placement' village in the early 19th century, and his vision has remained largely unspoilt to the present day. Starting at the 18th century rectory at one end of the village and walking all the way to the 17th century Quarry

Hill House at the other, it is not hard to imagine that you have stepped back in time to Tudor England. Besides the Castle, perhaps the most memorable building here is the magnificent church, which completely escaped 19th century restoration and features a splendid rood screen, pulpit, ceiling and pews.

Quarry Hill House

The Railway Walk continues to **Brandon**, only a short distance from Durham, or you can link into the seven-mile Deerness Valley Walk, an equally attractive way back to Crook, making this an ideal way to explore this part of the county. A good network of local bus services in the area makes it possible to return to a parked car without undue difficulty. These Railway Walks are two of several developed by the County Council in recent years, and leaflets, available from Tourist Information Centres, give full details.

The **Uplands Hotel**, on Acacia Gardens in Crook, was built as a domestic residence in the early 1900s, and, although it was converted to use as a pub as early as 1947, it still retains the look of a large detached private home.

Roy and Margaret Compton, the owners, offer comfortable five-bedroom accommodation and excellent cooking; Roy is a trained chef who makes good use of home-grown vegetables and other fresh local produce. The hotel has a formal dining-room but also serves interesting bar meals - Roy's 'specials' include Hot Cob, a bread bun filled with garlic sausage and baked in a rich cheese sauce, and Smokey Pot, pieces of bacon pan-fried with mushrooms, flamed in brandy and thickened with cream: delicious!

Children are welcomed at Uplands (particularly for the four-course traditional Sunday lunch) and the proprietors will gladly provide a baby-listening service for residents on request. The hotel also caters for wedding parties, private dinners and other functions, providing for gentle activity the use of a nine-hole putting green.

Uplands Hotel

Overlooking the River Wear itself is **Witton-le-Wear**, a village which terraces down the hillside, notable for its handsome green, its open views, attractive cottages and the old Dun Cow Inn with a datestone of 1799 above the door. The grounds of Witton Castle, a medieval fortified house just across the river, are now open to the public and, as well as walks through the parkland, there are swimming and paddling pools, refreshments, a games room, a shop and day fishing.

If you travel eastwards along the A689 from Bishop Auckland across County Durham, you reach **Sedgefield**, another particularly lovely village with a 13th century church, old coaching inns, Georgian houses and an extensive village green. Nearby is Hardwick Hall Country Park, an area of parkland and landscaped gardens now being developed by the County Council for recreation and conservation interest. Birdlife to be seen on the huge lake includes mallard, dabchick, moorhen, coot and, occasionally, heron and kingfisher. There are lakeside walks, a bird hide, nature trails and over 88 species of trees.

Natural beauty of an exceptional kind is also to be found near **Peterlee,** a purpose-built and planned 'New Town', created during the 1950s out of a huddle of mining villages around **Easington**. It was named in honour of an outstanding Durham miner and councillor, Peter Lee (1864-1935), who fought all his life for the well-being of the local community.

Castle Eden Dene Nature Reserve, on the south side of the town, is of national importance, being one of the largest woodlands in the North-East which has not been planted or extensively altered by man. It covers some 500 acres and lies in a steep-sided valley on magnesian limestone, with a wide variety of native trees and shrubs, wild flowers, birdlife and butterflies, including many rare insects. There is a network of footpaths to follow, some steep and narrow; visitors are requested to keep to paths at all time to avoid damage. It is managed by the Nature Conservancy Council and it makes sense to begin a visit at the Reserve Centre at Oakerside Dene Lodge on Stanhope Chase, off Durham Way in Peterlee, where leaflets and information are available.

A few miles further up the coast from Peterlee is **Seaham**, a much earlier 'New Town' that was developed by Lord Byron's family, the Londonderrys. In 1821 they bought what was then the old village of Seaham lock, stock and barrel, for the sole purpose of building a harbour from which to transport coal from the family's collieries to London and the Continent. The present town grew up around the harbour, and although most of the inland collieries have since closed, Seaham is still very much a working town and continues to exploit the reserves beneath the North Sea.

In the centre of town and just a short distance from the harbour, you will find a house called **'Adolphus'**. Margaret Vick, who recently returned from America where she had lived and worked for 28 years, found the house in a near derelict state. It was built in 1890 on land owned by the Marquis of Londonderry, who actually had the road built as a thoroughfare so that his guests could visit him here! Number 14 was originally owned by a rather well-to-do publican, who no doubt bought it as an investment. It is interesting that his family name was Thompson, and the Vick maternal grandparents were Thompsons from England. It would make a neat historical twist if we could state that Margaret is distantly related to the original owner, but that fact has not been verified. Margaret has all the deeds of the five previous owners in her safekeeping, which must make for interesting reading.

She is now putting a lot of energy into restoring the house to its former Victorian glory, and in the meantime still finds time to offer bed and breakfast facilities. The accommodation with full English breakfast is very moderately priced, and an evening meal is available on request. Margaret prides herself on her diverse cooking styles, much of it picked up whilst living abroad, so you can choose to eat English, American, and vegetarian cuisine, as well as pastry dishes which are her speciality. This is definitely a place where all tastes are catered for!

'Adolphus'

All that now remains of the original village is the 900-year-old church of St Mary and its vicarage, and Seaham Hall on the northern outskirts of town. Now a hotel, this was once the home of the Milbanke family, where in 1815 Lord Byron met and married Anne Isabella Milbanke - a marriage that was only to last for one year. You will find a large clifftop car park near the hotel with steps leading down to the beach, and here the rocky outcrops to the north of the harbour give way to miles of firm sand.

Dotheboys Hall, Bowes

Teesdale

Egglestone Abbey

CHAPTER THREE

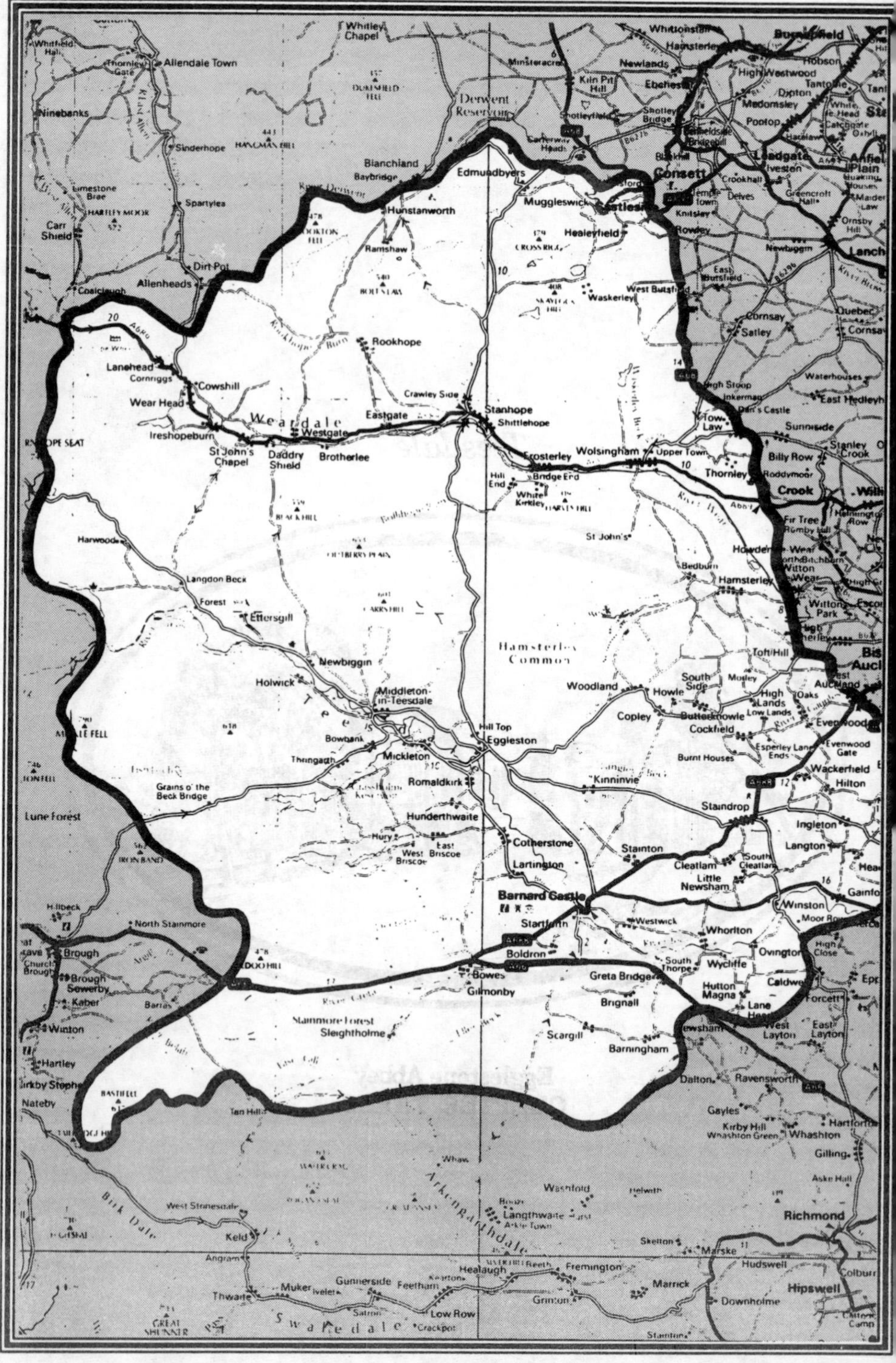

Whitley Chapel
Allendale Town
Ninebanks
Derwent Reservoir
Blanchland
Edmundbyers
Consett
Muggleswick
Hunstanworth
Healeyfield
Ramshaw
Allenheads
Rookhope
Waskerley
Lanehead
Cowshill
Wear Head
Weardale
Westgate
Eastgate
Stanhope
St John's Chapel
Daddry Shield
Brotherlee
Frosterley
Wolsingham
Tow Law
Crook
Harwood
Langdon Beck
Forest
Ettersgill
Newbiggin
Holwick
Middleton-in-Teesdale
Hamsterley Common
Hamsterley
Woodland
Copley
Eggleston
Mickleton
Romaldkirk
Hunderthwaite
Cotherstone
Lartington
Barnard Castle
Staindrop
Startforth
Boldron
Bowes
Gilmonby
Greta Bridge
Brignall
Lune Forest
Brough
Kaber
Winton
Hartley
Stainmore Forest
Sleightholme
Scargill
Barningham
Tan Hill
Keld
Muker
Gunnerside
Swaledale
Reeth
Fremington
Richmond
Hipswell
Arkengarthdale

Chapter Three - Map Reference Guide
Teesdale

The Bowes Museum - Barnard Castle

Mickleton Mill Caravan Park - Mickleton

The Shooting Lodge - Egglestone

Hetherick Caravan Park - Kinninvie

Park End Farm - Holwick

Teesdale Hotel - Middleton in Teesdale

Snaisgill Farm - Middleton in Teesdale

Thwaite Hall - Cotherstone

The Ancient Unicorn - Bowes

The Coach House - Whorlton

The Red Wel Inn - Barnard Castle

Gazebo House - Staindrop

Brunswick House - Middleton in Teesdale

Low Green - Mickleton

Brock Scar Cottage - Kelton

Quakers' Rest - Staindrop

Holme House - Piercebridge

High Force

CHAPTER THREE

Teesdale

People still argue as to whether or not Teesdale is really the last of the Yorkshire Dales or the first of the Durham Dales. Until 1974 much of the River Tees actually formed the Yorkshire-Durham county boundary, with the south bank claimed by the North Riding of Yorkshire, the north bank by County Durham.

The recent designation of much of the dale as part of the new North Pennines Area of Outstanding Natural Beauty has resolved the argument. Above any difference of opinion is the fact that Teesdale is an area of quite exceptional, intimate beauty, both natural and man-made, reflecting qualities of both the softer landscape of the Yorkshire Dales to the south, and the austere grandeur of the North Pennine uplands to the north.

Barnard Castle is a natural focal point for any exploration of the central parts of Teesdale. This old market town owes its existence to the castle founded in 1112 by one Bernard, son of Guy de Baliol, one of the knights who fought alongside the Conqueror. The ruins, with the massive, round keep overlooking the town's narrow, arched bridge over the Tees, have a gaunt beauty; and the castle has experienced its share of incident, perhaps most spectacularly during the ill-fated Catholic Rising of the North in 1569. At that time it was besieged by rebel forces for 11 days and, although it was finally forced to capitulate, this gave sufficient time for Queen Elizabeth's army, under the Earl of Sussex, to speed to York and force the rebels to flee. Many were executed and those leading families who had supported the plans to replace Elizabeth with Mary Queen of Scots lost their lands.

The town has an especially rich architectural heritage, with handsome houses, cottages, shops and inns dating from the 16th to the 19th centuries. There is an impressive market cross and an old town hall contained within an unusual octagonal structure, built by one Thomas Breaks in 1747, the area under the verandah having been used as a butter-market and the upstairs variously as a lock-up or courthouse. You can still see the bullet holes in the weather-vane, resulting from a wager by two local men in 1804, shooting from outside the Turk's Head, 100 yards away, to determine who was the best shot. History does not record the winner.

Blagraves House, on The Bank, dates from the early 16th century and was most probably the inn at which Oliver Cromwell stayed, on 24th October 1648, when he came to the town and was given mulled wine and shortcake by the townspeople. At the junction of Newgate and The Bank is the plaque which marks the site of the shop used by Charles Dickens in his story 'Master Humphrey's Clock'. An excellent town trail is available from the Tourist Information Centre in Galgate.

A short walk along Newgate will bring you to **The Bowes Museum**, a magnificent building designed by Jules Pellechet in the style of a French chateau. John Bowes, son of the 10th Earl of Strathmore, and his French actress wife, Josephine, spent 15 years putting together remarkable collections of artifacts, intending that the public should be able to see and enjoy them. This was the purpose of the building which, after taking about 30 years to build, was completed in 1892.

The Bowes Museum

A strong European influence is evident throughout the museum, both in the ceramic and textile displays and in the period settings in which are exhibited the furniture, tapestries, paintings, clocks and objets d'art. Displays have been added more recently featuring English furniture, silver, costume, toys and local antiquities. Sadly, by the time the museum was opened both Bowes and his wife were dead. Her Majesty Queen Elizabeth The Queen Mother, who was born Lady Elizabeth Bowes-Lyon, is descended from the Bowes family.

The museum, now owned by Durham County Council, houses these outstanding collections, which are nationally important and include paintings by Goya and El Greco, in surroundings that have been called 'The Taj Mahal of the North-East'.

Unusually, the **Red Well Inn** at Barnard Castle is co-hosted by Mike and Liz Rudd, and Ken and Anne Thompson - which means that guests can be assured a total of four warm welcomes instead of the normal two! This traditional country inn, resplendent with ivy, offers guests a really comfortable place to rest and relax. The accommodation is of a particularly high standard, the en-suite bedrooms having been furnished to the Toursit Board '4 Crowns' classification. There is a function room suitable for wedding receptions and parties, two rooms available for business meetings, and a dance floor with disco facilities - in short, your hosts will provide you with just about anything you require. With recommendations from CAMRA and the Good Food Guide, their slogan 'Ale's well - that's Red Well' says it all!

The Red Well Inn

Those visitors with a caravan in tow will, with a little bit of perseverance, find a splendid park near by. 'Keep right on to the end of the road.....' go the words of that familiar First World War song, and to find **Hetherick Caravan Park,** you may well have to do just that! As you take the road north from Barnard Castle to **Kinninvie**, you will easily spot the display board with flags that leads you onto a small track which seems to go on forever.

The drive certainly gives you a good opportunity to enjoy this open farmland, and the peaceful park with flowing streams and plenty of trees is a very attractive spot indeed. The 10-acre site opened as recently as March 1991, and with an adjacent seven-acre stand of woodland close by, walkers and lovers of wildlife will have plenty to see and do. Full amenities include a spacious amenity block with W.C.s, hot and cold water and shaver points, as well as laundry facilities, a shop and a children's play area. A lot of effort and care has gone into landscaping the area to provide a harmonious caravan site. There are 86 pitches for caravans, and 11 independent pitches for tourers with electric hook-up points. If you have a motor tourer or a tent, you are still very welcome to make use of the site.

Mr Holmes, the owner of the site, is fast improving and expanding the facilities, so by the time you read this even more caravans are likely to be in place. It would appear that Durham Council are not too keen on seeing caravans from the road, but ultimately this works to everyone's advantage. Hetherick is so far from the road that it would be difficult to imagine a more quiet and peaceful spot - and this of course is the main reason people come here!

Hetherick Caravan Park

Egglestone Abbey, about a mile and a half to the south-east of Barnard Castle and easily reached by riverside footpath, is quite different in character to the The Bowes Museum - the ruins of a Cistercian Abbey of which most of the nave, built in the 13th and 14th century, survives. This was only a small monastic settlement but it enjoys a superb setting above the River Tees.

You'll find grandeur to rival The Bowes Museum, however, at Raby Castle, some seven miles north-east of Barnard Castle on the A688 and near the charming village of **Staindrop.**

Raby is one of England's grandest medieval castles, in a magnificent setting of parkland, lake and gardens; a romantic, fairy-tale building which was the home of the Nevill family, powerful northern barons, until it was siezed by the Crown after the Nevills' involvement in the abortive Rising of the North. Much of the interior is now Georgian and Victorian, though the Great Kitchen remains virtually unaltered after 600 years. There are collections of fine furniture and paintings, including masterpieces by Sir Peter Lely and Sir Joshua Reynolds and a coach house with a collection of carriages.

Staindrop itself is a delightful, very typical, traditional Durham village, linear in form and with extensive village greens. It is very much an estate village which evolved to serve Raby Castle. It has a number of fine Georgian houses and attractive cottages, a 16th century manor house and a church that dates back to Saxon times, with a Norman tower and some remarkable medieval tombstone effigies of the Nevills.

While we were in the village we discovered two fascinating houses in North Green, both offering excellent accommodation facilities and a wealth of character and history.

Tucked quietly away in the corner of a row of houses in the centre of the village, you will find an original Quakers' Meeting House. **Quakers' Rest** is today a charming private house, where Rose and Ray Hill offer bed and breakfast accommodation and let out their adjoining holiday cottage. Externally, the building has changed very little since its Meeting House days, but it has been completely rebuilt inside and offers guests extremely comfortable surroundings and all modern conveniences.

And yet, behind its initial appearance as simply a charming bed and breakfast establishment with an interesting history, Quakers' Rest has a secret to tell. When the Hills bought the property some 10 years ago, the garden was a real jungle. As the couple began the arduous task of clearing it, they found to their amazement that the garden was actually a cemetery - complete with 18 headstones! They have now transformed it into a true haven of peace and tranquillity, cleverly designing it around the stones so as not to disturb them.

Several of the stones bear the name 'Dixon', of Mason-Dixon Line fame, and this in itself would make Quakers' Rest a popular tourist attraction if the Hills decided to broadcast the fact widely. However, full marks must go to Rose and Ray for maintaining the restful atmosphere of this strange garden despite the improvements they have made, and for keeping it low key. So hidden a secret is this place, that many of the locals know nothing of the true story behind it and are completely unaware of the existence of the headstones. They do occasionally allow visitors to view it, but out of respect for both the Hills and their permanent 'residents', we feel it best that you view the garden by staying at the house for a day or two or renting the cottage if you wish to stay longer.

Quakers' Rest

Near by, we found **Gazebo House** - and what a find it was! This is Bed and Breakfast accommodation in really splendid surroundings. The main house, where owners Mr and Mrs Shingler live, is part of a Georgian terrace. The house is double fronted with an elegant white facade, and meals can be taken in the conservatory. There is a delightful walled garden to stroll in and here you will find the Gazebo that gives the house its name. An absolutely charming 18th century building, it boasts its own tower and here guests can take tea and admire the surroundings. With flagged pathways, abundant shrubs and mellow stone walls, Gazebo House is quite lovely. The Shinglers have two guest rooms in the main house, one overlooking the village green and one overlooking the garden. They are a charming couple who really make you feel that you are visiting old friends, and with such treats as homemade bread to enjoy, your stay is certain to be very comfortable.

Gazebo House

You could not be better placed for visiting Raby Castle; indeed, the house backs onto the park. Staindrop can also claim a rather distinguished 'resident' in a churchyard, the Royal Surveyor Jeremiah Dixon, who went to America with his English colleague Charles Mason. There in the Deep South, they drew that 'ole Mason-Dixon Line'! And nearly a thousand years ago, Staindrop was a little capital - the home of King Cnut, 'Emperor of the North'.

The Gazebo

Lovers of romantic landscape should make their way south of Barnard Castle to Greta Bridge on the A66, the old hump-backed bridge immortalised in paintings by the great English water-colourists Girtin, Turner and others, now bypassed by the traffic on the trunk road. Footpaths lead by the riverside, through the edge of Rokeby Park, past the famous and often painted 'Meeting of the Waters' where the Greta joins the Tees, to the ruins of medieval Mortham Tower, subject of Sir Walter Scott's narrative poem of colourful chivalry and courtly love, 'Rokeby'. The elegant Palladian house, where Scott stayed to write his poem, is open to the public during the summer months.

Greta Bridge

This is a beautiful, little known landscape of mid-Teesdale; undulating countryside of scattered woods and old farms, through which lanes wind to such villages as **Barningham, Hutton Magna, Whorlton** and **Gainford,** the latter with a rare 17th century circular beehive dovecote in the garden of the hall, visible from the road.

A warm welcome awaits you at **The Coach House**, a converted stable which can be found in the tiny, picturesque village of **Whorlton**. Situated on the banks of the River Tees, three miles east of Barnard Castle, the house stands in charming well-stocked gardens, and guests can be assured of a peaceful and tranquil stay here. There are two double bedrooms available with a private sitting room with tea and coffee making facilities, a colour television and a bathroom for the exclusive use of guests. A Full English Breakfast is served, and proprietor Helen Calder is happy to provide an evening meal if required. If you would prefer a vegetarian meal, do please let Mrs Calder know. The River Tees is just a few minutes walk away, and this is an area rich in birdlife. Birds such as Herons, Dippers and

Mallards can be seen as you stroll along the riverbank, and if you are very lucky, you may spot a Kingfisher as it flashes by.

The Coach House

If you carry on along the A67 east of Gainsford, you will find the historic village of **Piercebridge** with its picturesque, whitewashed cottages, just off the main road. The village green is the site of a Roman fort which once guarded the bridge where Dere Street crossed the River Tees. Sand and gravel quarrying unearthed the remarkably well-preserved remains of a second Roman bridge to the east of the village, illustrating how much the Tees has changed its course over the centuries. In the main street is the George Hotel, the setting of that once-popular song, 'My Grandfather's Clock', where 'the clock stopped, never to go again'. This recalls the time when the George was run by the Jenkins brothers during the 19th century. When one of them died, the long-case clock in the hall started to lose time, and at the precise moment of the other brother's death - 4.46 - it stopped for ever.

If you are looking for somewhere to stay for a night or two after visiting Piercebridge and its famous Roman remains, we recommend that you make your way to **Holme House.** When you leave the village heading south towards Richmond on the B6275, you will come to a sharp bend to the right, with a small lane on your left. Take this lane, over two cattle grids, bearing right down the gravelled drive, and there you will find Holme House. This elegant 18th century farmhouse is set in 350 acres of mixed farmland, with a large garden for guests to enjoy. We were particularly taken with the walled kitchen garden area, which is wonderfully secluded and provides the Grahams with a lot of their fresh vegetables.

Even though your stay here may be brief, you will immediately be made to feel part of the family in the relaxed, informal atmosphere of this lovely home. The accommodation consists of two comfortable twin bedded rooms with private bathroom, but your lasting impression of Holme House is bound to be the hearty English or Continental breakfast which greets you when you wake refreshed in the morning. Well used to feeding a busy farming family, Anne Graham enjoys a challenge and healthy appetites are her forte! As for your lunch and evening meal, there are a host of excellent hotels and pubs in the surrounding villages, and the Grahams will be happy to make their recommendations if you need help choosing a suitable venue.

Holme House

For a short but spectacular drive into the Yorkshire Dales from Barnard Castle, take the steep and narrow road, reached south of the A66 to Reeth and Arkengarthdale, which crosses over Stang Pass through Stang Forest. A car park above the forest gives access to Hope Scar from where there are panoramic views across County Durham, as far, on a clear day, as Durham Cathedral and the Cleveland coast.

The main A66 trunk road westwards from Barnard Castle heads across the Stainmoor Pass, following the line of the Roman Road towards Carlisle. The old coaching town of **Bowes** once enjoyed notoriety as the location of Bowes Academy, kept by one William Shaw, which was visited by Dickens in 1838 and upon which he subsequently based Dotheboys Hall in his novel 'Nicholas Nickelby'. George Ashton Taylor, a youth who died in 1822 at the age of 19 and is buried in the village churchyard, was the inspiration for the character, Smike, in the book. 'I think his ghost put Smike into my head, upon the spot', Dickens later reported to a friend. Taylor had been a pupil at the very 'Academy' that Dickens would so mercilessly expose, and it is a testament to the extraordinary power of the author's words that, within a few years of the publication of the novel, pupils were being withdrawn and the notorious Yorkshire schools were fast being driven out of business.

As a name for an inn, the **Ancient Unicorn** certainly conjures up some interesting ideas! To be found in the quiet village street at Bowes, it was originally a 16th century coaching inn. One can imagine the coaches drawing up to the building, pulled by rather weary unicorns! Dickens is said to have wined and dined here whilst researching material for his novel, and we are sure that the excellent range of beers, ales and bar food, coupled with the friendly atmosphere, would satisfy even Mr Pickwick himself! Accommodation currently consists of four bedrooms each with private bathroom, and three self-catering cottages will hopefully be available by the summer of 1992.

Bowes Castle was completed in 1187 for King Henry II, using stone from an earlier Roman fort, Lavatrae, to guard this strategic crossing of the Pennines. Its massive keep still overlooks the River Greta, but much of the castle's stone was re-used by thrifty local people to build the parish church. This is wild, bleak countryside. The main A66 trunk road crosses Stainmoor over desolate moorland and is often closed during the first snows of winter, leaving drivers stranded in Bowes or Brough. It was near this road, close to the present Cumbria border, that King Edmund erected Rey Cross to mark the boundary between Northumbria and what was then the Scottish province of Cumbria. It also marks the spot where Eric Bloodaxe, last Viking king of Northumbria, was slain.

Teesdale, north of Barnard Castle, is very different to this austere trans-Pennine pass. Between Barnard Castle and Middleton, the dale narrows and becomes more intimate, lushly wooded. There are delightful walks close to, or alongside, the river, past such villages as Cotherstone, with the remains of its castle, and the delightful Romaldkirk, named after its church of St Romald, son of a king of Northumbria who, miraculously, could speak at birth but only lived three days. There is a series of village greens surrounded by cottages of great character, a village pump and two pubs.

We found two delightful self-catering cottages at **Thwaite Hall** on the outskirts of **Cotherstone**. Owner Irene Suckling makes a point of stating that they are very comprehensively equipped, and this is no exaggeration. It is rare to come across a self-catering establishment where visitors need only bring themselves! From toiletries to kitchen towels, all else is provided. Beds are made up for your arrival, and if chilly, the fire lit. The cottages stand on a rise just outside the village which is only 5-10 minutes walk away, as is the river. Gentle walks abound in the immediate area, while what Wainwright describes as the most beautiful part of the Pennine Way is nearby.

Though centrally situated in the Dale, this is a haven of peace. Both cottages look out over the lawn to fields and hills - one leading directly to a walled garden. Beautiful old stone warms gently in the sun with nothing but a late pheasant or early owl to disturb the still evening air. Bird life is prolific, but there is a paddock specifically designated for dogs where they can be exercised. Mrs Suckling stresses that the customer is all-important here: this is THEIR holiday and she is here to give whatever help they may require to make sure they come to love Teesdale as much as she does. To receive a brochure giving full details of Thwaite Hall, please telephone Teesdale 50782.

Thwaite Hall

Eggleston, a former lead-mining village, lies higher up the dale. Eggleston Hall Gardens are open to visitors and include a walled garden where rare plants and organically grown vegetables are for sale.

We discovered **The Shooting Lodge** at **High Shipley**, a working farm just off the B6278 south of Eggleston. Situated in an area known locally as the 'secret dale', this historic lodge stands high on a hill with views over the River Tees. Very much off the beaten track, this area is outstanding for its beauty and solitude. Dating back to Tudor times, the Lodge was thought to have been one of Richard III's hunting lodges and the story goes that it was used as 'payment' to Miles Forest in 1484 for his dastardly part in the murder of the King's nephews.

The owner, Mrs Gill, has lovingly restored the Lodge and today guests can enjoy beautifully appointed self-catering accommodation here. Sleeping nine people in all, the Lodge has a wealth of original features including mullion windows with leaded lights, oak beams, flagged floors and a marvellous inglenook fireplace in the lounge. As a point of architectural interest, we were intrigued to discover that the stone roofing tiles are held in place with sheep bones!

In addition to the Lodge itself, there is also a very comfortable cottage available which sleeps four. The facilities in both the Lodge and the cottage are excellent, and all fuel and power is included in the rental charge. High Shipley is ideally positioned for exploring a wealth of nearby attractions, and those of you looking for a truly peaceful and relaxing holiday will find this a memorable experience.

The Shooting Lodge

Several Neolithic burial sites have been discovered around the stone village of **Mickleton,** which lies two miles to the south-east of Middleton on the B6277. As you approach the village from the direction of Barnard Castle, do look out for the driveway leading to **Low Green farmhouse**. Here you will find very attractive accommodation in the 200-year-old barn, which has been converted to provide two double rooms and a family suite, with a spacious kitchen and breakfast room below. Judy Dixon provides a full English breakfast, and packed lunches and an evening meal can be arranged in any of the local inns in the area. Low Green is a lovely stone dwelling standing in seven acres of fine grounds on the south bank of the River Tees. Although Judy and her family moved in comparatively recently in 1983, the previous family had lived there continuously since the house was built - a record that we are sure the Dixons would like to match! Do note that guests are requested to refrain from smoking, and as the accommodation has proved very popular it would be advisable to make your reservation by phone. The number is (0833) 40425.

Low Green

Accommodation of a different kind in this part of the lovely, rolling Durham Dales can be found at **Mickleton Mill Caravan Park**. This is an ideal base for visitors to explore the Tees Valley and enjoy a host of local activities such as sailing, horse-riding, canoeing and windsurfing. The park also has private fishing available for residents on the River Lune, which flows along one side of the site. Owners Keith and Carole Atkinson have provided a wonderfully tranquil setting for their guests and the pitches have been positioned to afford a good deal of privacy. There are pitches for both static and touring caravans, mains electricity is laid on and there are two toilet blocks with showers and hot water. The large recreational area makes this a perfect place for those with children.

To find Mickleton Mill Caravan Park, take the turning opposite Mickleton post office which is in the centre of the village. The park is open from April to October.

Mickleton Mill Caravan Park

Some three miles to the south-west, nestled in the surrounding hills at Kelton with Grassholme Reservoir only a short walk away, you will find **Brock Scar Cottage.**

Brock Scar Cottage

The cottage has been recently renovated and offers guests an idyllic setting for a holiday in this lovely part of Durham. Ian and Wyn Gargate have spent a long time restoring this old dwelling to turn it into a comfortable home with all the modern amenities. The electrics and mains were installed just two years ago and if you are a D.I.Y. enthusiast, it's worth taking a look at the photographs taken by Ian to appreciate the amount of labour that went into the renovation. The happy result is a delightful and extremely cosy place which you are sure to love.

The letters 'R.R.' and a date of 1853 are carved above the door. Ian told us that this probably referred to a previous renovation project - 'Re-Renovated' - so the cottage could be far older than the date initially suggests. It is rather nice to think of an earlier young couple moving in with exciting plans for the future of their newly acquired cottage! The cottage is totally self-contained, but Wyn and Ian live nearby and are always close at hand if you need advice on where to go, what to do, or where to eat!

Middleton-in-Teesdale, the capital of Upper Teesdale, is a small, grey town in a dramatically beautiful setting with the Tees running below, while all around is a great backcloth of green hills. The town's links with the lead-mining industry are apparent in the Market Square, where there is a handsome cast-iron fountain which was purchased and placed there, in 1875, by the employees of the Quaker-owned London Lead Mining Company. The expense was covered from subscriptions raised for the retirement of the company's local superintendent, Robert Bainbridge.

Dieter and Audrey Streit greet all their guests with a warm and friendly welcome at the spacious **Teesdale Hotel** in the Market Square. This fine old coaching inn was built from warm mellow stone, and has a rather grand air about it as you sweep through the arched gateway. Passing through the courtyard, we spotted some murals by local artist Cacan Corrigan, depicting Middleton as it must have been many centuries ago! This is a very lavish yet cosy hotel, where your feet sink into thick carpets and the furnishings are designed to make you feel as if you had never left home.

The beamed restaurant, which is open to non-residents, offers a superb menu and you can enjoy morning coffee and bar lunches, or dine a la carte. As this was once a coaching inn, you will be pleased to know that parking proves no problem, with ample space within the courtyard. There are 14 bedrooms in all, most with private bathroom, and if you would prefer to stay in self-catering accommodation, there are four charming terraced cottages to let within the courtyard. Previously used for stabling, the cottages have all been individually designed and tastefully furnished and provide a superb range of amenities.

Everything has been done to make your stay at the Teesdale as comfortable as possible, and Dieter and Audrey firmly believe that only a family run hotel can offer its guests the friendliness and personal attention they deserve. The lovely moors and the spectacular High Force waterfall are only a short drive away, and we can think of nothing better after busy day's touring than to return to the comfort and relaxing atmosphere of this charming hotel.

Teesdale Hotel

It is well worth having a wander down to the quieter end of the Market Place, where you will find a very pleasant Guest House and Tea Room called **Brunswick House.** It stands opposite St Mary's Church and offers tourists an ideal base from which to tour the surrounding area. When we were there, we noticed that coaches tend to arrive at the other end of town to drop off visitors, and we thought it would be a shame not to draw their attention to this super place, just a short walk away.

Middleton itself is a surprisingly elegant place, with many fine buildings including St Mary's Parish Church with its unusual detached bell tower. Prosperity came to the town through lead mining and the arrival of the London Lead Mining Company in 1815.

When the company established its northern headquarters in the town, wealth and livelihoods were assured.

Quieter by far today, visitors will enjoy discovering this gem of a town, and Brunswick House would be the perfect place to stay. Dating back to 1760, it is a charming residence with four attractively furnished bedrooms offering full modern amenities. In the tea room, guests and non-residents can enjoy tasty meals, traditional afternoon teas, or just a coffee and a slice of cake, all homemade from the best of local produce. If you are planning a day out during your stay, do ask the proprietors Sheila and Andrew Milnes about a packed lunch, which they will happily provide.

Brunswick House

Although the lead-mining industry disappeared over 80 years ago, Middleton still has the strong feeling of being a mining town, with company-built houses, shops, offices and sober chapels to keep the population suitably moral in outlook. The surrounding hills are still pockmarked with remains of old workings, spoil-heaps and deep, and often dangerous, shafts; but the town's agricultural links remain strong, with streets still known as Market Place, Market Cross and Cattle Market. Like Barnard Castle, it is increasing in popularity as a centre from which to explore both Teesdale and the entire North Pennines.

If you are looking for farmhouse accommodation in the Middleton area, do give Susan Parmley a ring at **Snaisgill Farm**. Situated in 30 acres of land in secluded, peaceful surroundings, her lovely 19th century farmhouse provides all the comforts of a home from home and would make an ideal base for touring the Weardales. There are two good sized bedrooms, a cosy resident's lounge with colour television, and the house is centrally heated throughout. The farmhouse breakfasts are simply tremendous - both in size and in quality - and no one could leave Susan's table feeling less than satisfied! Children are most welcome and prices are very reasonable.

Susan also has a self-catering cottage on the site, and although this is almost permanently booked, it may well be worth telephoning her if you are planning a longer stay in the area. Do ring first in any event, as in addition

to looking after her guests, Susan is also busy helping run the farm. The number is (0833) 40343. To find Snaisgill Farm, take the road out of Middleton, following signs to Weardale. Ignore the turning to Stanhope and carry on up the road until you come to the third farm along. You have arrived!

Snaisgill Farm

Middleton is also the centre for some magnificent walks in Upper Teesdale. The most famous of these is The Pennine Way on its 250-mile route from Derbyshire and Yorkshire to the Cheviots and the Scottish Border. It enters Middleton and Teesdale from the bleak yet beautiful landscapes of Baldersdale and Lunesdale, with their chains of moorland reservoirs and scattered hill-farms.

From Middleton northwards, though, the path follows a much gentler route, past flower-rich meadows which turn vivid gold, white and blue in late Spring, past traditional, whitewashed farmsteads and spectacular, riverside scenery, including Holwick Scars, the thrilling waterfalls at Low Force and High Force and on to Cauldron Snout. This section of The Pennine Way is as scenically fine as anything to be found along the whole route. It is an area famous throughout England for its wild flowers, including the lovely tri-coloured Teesdale Pansy, vivid in both pastureland and meadowland in late May and early June. It is also an excellent area in which to enjoy a variety of birdlife. Among birds to be found are golden plovers, dippers, and the ubiquitous curlew, with kestrels hanging in the sky above rocky scars.

The traditional stone cottage at **Park End Farm** in **Holwick** has been refurbished to a very high standard, and offers excellent self-catering accommodation with fine views of the surrounding countryside. The road through the village to the farm ends in a cul-de-sac, so you can be assured of a peaceful break. Your friendly host is Mr Raine, who has gone to a lot of trouble to make the property comfortable for his guests. The cottage is absolutely ideal for disabled guests, incorporating ramp access and a downstairs toilet and shower. The modern kitchen has every facility you are likely to need, and the lounge features a woodburning stove to make you feel really cosy. Holwick is really no more than a hamlet (although it does have its own pub!) so this is definitely a place for those who are weary of noise and stress. Having said that, Park End Farm is ideally situated for touring further afield when you want to do something more energetic than simply relaxing.

Park End Farm

Of course, you don't have to be a Pennine Way walker to enjoy all that Upper Teesdale has to offer. A choice of shorter, circular walks can be devised to take advantage of this scenically magnificent part of the dale; for example, from Bowlees car park, picnic area and excellent Visitor Centre, about three-and-a-half miles from Middleton on the Bowes road. There are four small waterfalls within this area and an impressive waterfall-concealed cave nearby - Gibson's Cave. The walk continues to High Force itself, one of the finest and most impressive waterfalls anywhere in England, returning along the riverside, crossing a tiny suspension bridge, Wynch Bridge, to Bowlees. Leaflets of recommended walks are to be found in the Visitor

Centre at Bowlees or at Barnard Castle Tourist Information Centre, where local Ordnance Survey Maps, indicating rights of way, are on sale.

No visitor to Teesdale can afford to miss High Force. In spate it is a breathtaking sight - twin surges of creamy-white, peat-stained water thundering over 60ft through and over a great wall of dark, volcanic whinstone rock, the roar of water echoing along and across the valley to be heard miles away. Ancient juniper trees grow out of the crags around the falls, heightening the dramatic effect. A car park and picnic site, on the opposite side of the main Alston road, are conveniently positioned with an easy footway to view the falls. Keep to the main paths, as the rocks and pools can be extremely slippery and currents dangerously deep and strong.

Still following The Pennine Way, the more adventurous can make their way close by Cronkley Scar and Falcon Clints, and Widdybank Fell, an internationally important nature reserve famous for Spring Gentians, to where Cauldron Spout, described as England's largest cascade, roars down from Cow Green Reservoir. Beyond here The Pennine Way crosses bleak country into Cumbria, past Maizebeck and Dufton Fell to High Cup Nick, in the Eden Valley, a route only to be attempted in clear weather by well-equipped walkers using large-scale maps. Not far from the path lie military ranges with restricted access. You can, however, drive to the car park and picnic-site at Cow Green via the back road from Langdon Beck (signposted) via Peghorn and the reservoir track, from where there is a Nature Trail down to Cauldron Spout - leaflets are available.

From High Force the road leads past Langdon Beck, across high moorland passes, to Alston and to St John's Chapel in Weardale, both thrilling drives with extensive views across and down Upper Teesdale. In fine weather, there is no more impressive landscape to be enjoyed anywhere in England.

Northumbrian Cattle Shed

Weardale

The Fossil Tree, Stanhope Churchyard

CHAPTER FOUR

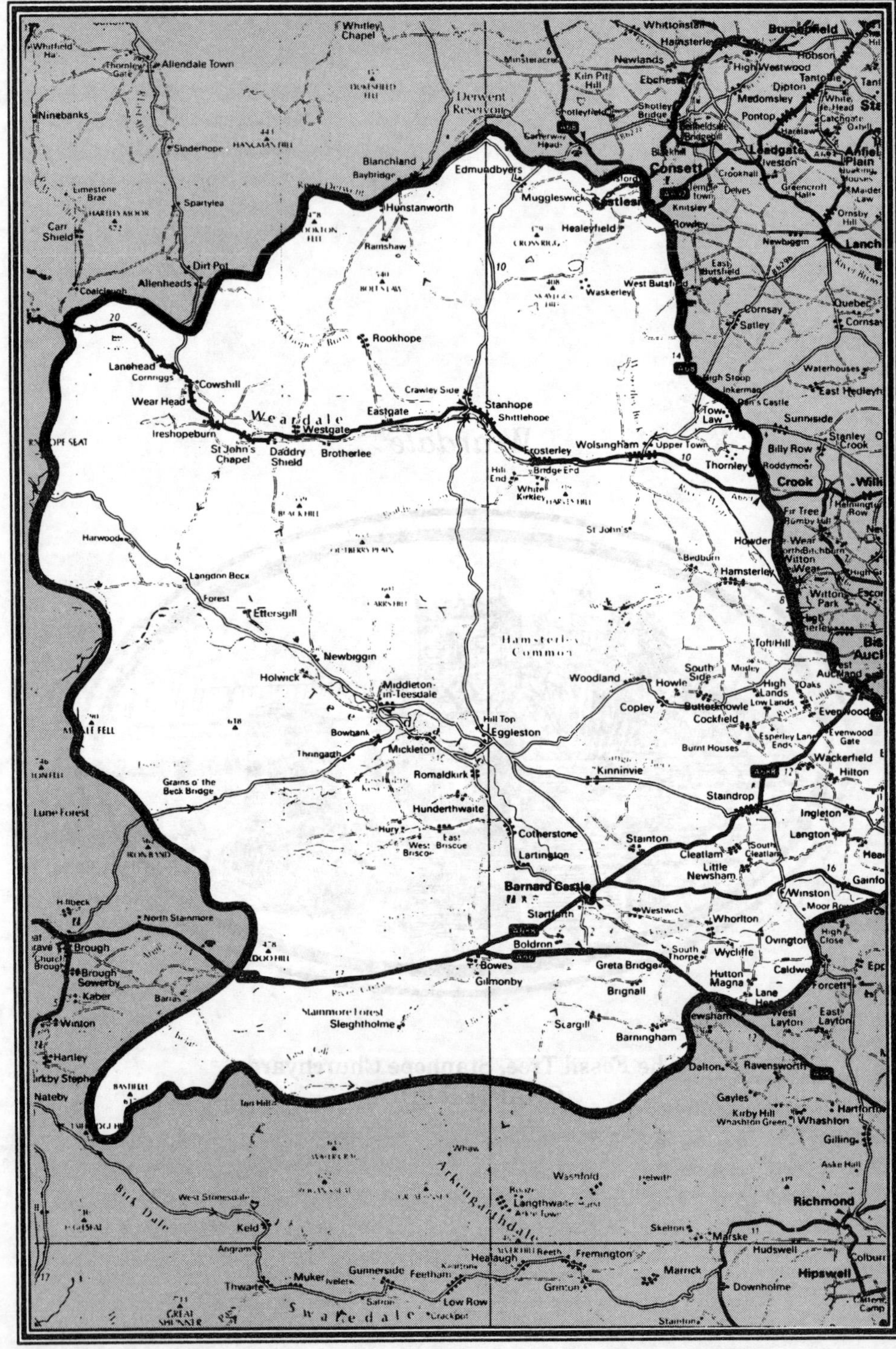

Whitley Chapel
Allendale Town
Ninebanks
Sinderhope
Spartylea
Carr Shield
Dirt Pot
Allenheads
Coalcleugh
Derwent Reservoir
Blanchland
Edmundbyers
Hunstanworth
Ramshaw
Rookhope
Muggleswick
Healeyfield
Waskerley
West Butsfield
Consett
Whittonstall
Hamsterley
Newlands
Ebchester
Medomsley
Dipton
Leadgate
Lanehead
Cowshill
Wear Head
Ireshopeburn
St John's Chapel
Daddry Shield
Westgate
Brotherlee
Eastgate
Weardale
Stanhope
Crawley Side
Frosterley
Wolsingham
Tow Law
Thornley
Crook
Harwood
Langdon Beck
Forest
Ettersgill
Newbiggin
Holwick
Middleton-in-Teesdale
Bowbank
Mickleton
Romaldkirk
Eggleston
Hunderthwaite
Cotherstone
Lartington
Hamsterley Common
Woodland
Copley
Cockfield
Staindrop
Barnard Castle
Startforth
Boldron
Bowes
Gilmonby
Greta Bridge
Brignall
Scargill
Barningham
Stainmore Forest
Sleightholme
Brough
Kaber
Winton
Hartley
Nateby
Keld
Muker
Gunnerside
Healaugh
Reeth
Fremington
Swaledale
Richmond

Chapter Four - Map Reference Guide
Weardale

Friarside Farm - Wolsingham

The Bonny Moor Hen - Stanhope

Rookhope Inn - Rookhope

Westgate House - Westgate-in-Weardale

Killhope Wheel Lead Mining Centre - Cowshill

Heatherside - Edmundbyers

Thistlewood Cottages - Wolsingham

Alston & Killhope Riding Centre - Cowshill

Lands Farm - Westgate-in-Weardale

The Park Horse Inn - Stanhope

Hamsterley Forest - Redford

Gazebo, at Bishop Oak Hall, Wolsingham

CHAPTER FOUR

Weardale

Compared with the pristine beauty of Teesdale, with its neat white-walled farmhouses and shimmering waterfalls, Weardale might, at first glance, seem an anticlimax. Yet this could not be further from the truth. Weardale has a character of its own. Perhaps the hills are not as high; the valley may be broader and less dramatic and this is very much a working valley with limestone quarries and the remains of lead and iron mining. One of the limestone quarries at Eastgate still supplies the steel works of Teesside by means of long train-loads which trundle along the surviving Weardale railway, through Stanhope and Bishop Auckland.

It is also a dale rich in human interest, a relatively heavily populated valley, with villages of typical, rugged Durham character which are there, not only for the tourist or the retired, but also for ordinary people, with pubs, shops and chapels, as well as the odd craft workshop.

Between and behind the villages, winding down to the river or up the fellsides, is a rich network of footpaths, making this a marvellous area for walking, away from the better known and more crowded areas of the Pennines. The villages between Cowshill and Stanhope are linked by quiet back lanes, ideal for cycling or for those who wish simply to take time to explore quiet and little-used byways.

Access by public transport is good, too. The little red-and-cream Weardale bus meanders up and down the valley every hour from **Bishop Auckland** and **Crook**, threading its way between such communities as **Tow Law, Wolsingham, Frosterley, Stanhope, Eastgate, Westgate, St John's Chapel,** and **Wearhead**, as far as the hamlet of **Cowshill**. Such a regular bus service makes it easy to plan a walk along or across the valley, returning to a parked car or back to base by bus.

During the summer, these buses link with a scenic train service on British Rail's Darlington-Bishop Auckland Heritage Line which, on Sundays, continues into Upper Weardale from Darlington and Bishop Auckland to the re-opened station at Stanhope. Buses meet the trains to take passengers on a spectacular journey, climbing to the head of the dale, past Killhope Wheel, before ascending past Weardale Forest and Killhope Cross, over 2,000ft above sea level, to Nenthead and Alston in Cumbria. This is England's highest bus route.

Whether you travel this road by bus or by car, the austere beauty and grandeur of the Upper Weardale landscape will soon impress you with a magic of its own. The bare, yet beautiful, Northern Pennine summits such as Burnhope Seat, Knoutberry Hill, Lamb's Head and Low Killhope, are the haunt of curlew, plover and kestrel.

In a hollow before the final ascent of the moorland pass to Nenthead, lies Killhope Mine, once a major undertaking at the heart of the northern Pennines lead-mining area which extends from Durham into Cumbria. The Pennines have been worked for their mineral riches, particularly lead, since Roman times but, until the 18th century, the industry remained relatively primitive and small scale. The development of new techniques of mechanisation, in the later 18th and early 19th century, allowed the industry to grow until it was second only to coal as a major extractive industry in the region. In 1860 the Beaumont Company installed at Killhope some of the newest technology then available, including a massive 33ft 8" overshot water-wheel, now the only surviving water-wheel still to drive crushing rollers.

Killhope lies at the heart of the northern lead-mining dales, a vast upland which was once the principal lead-mining area of Britain. Now the country's best-preserved lead-mining site and designated an ancient monument, Killhope Mine is the focal point of what is now the remarkable **Killhope Wheel Lead Mining Centre**, dominated by the famous water-wheel.

The wheel used moorland streams, feeding a small reservoir, to provide power for the lead-ore crushing mills, where galena (lead-ore) from the hillside mines was washed and crushed ready for smelting into pigs of lead. Much of the machinery has been carefully restored by Durham County Council together with part of the smelting mill, underground adits, workshops, a smithy, mine ponies and their stalls, tools, and miners' sleeping quarters to form part of a major Visitor Centre interpreting this once great industry of the Durham Dales. A fascinating museum and trail around the site explain the history and the processes which were used. The centre is located alongside the A689 Stanhope to Alston road, two-and-a-half miles west of Cowshill.

Killhope Wheel Lead Mining Centre

The real Weardale begins at **Cowshill** and at **Wearhead,** where the first cottages and hamlets merge to form villages and Killhope Burn joins the infant River Wear as it splashes its way down from Burnhope Reservoir on the moors above.

Janet Ellis runs the **Alston and Killhope Riding Centre at Low Cornriggs Farm** near Cowshill, and as she is an expert rider and tutor, you are in very safe hands. Janet and her fellow instructors are well used to the initial traumas of the novice rider, and if you have never ridden a horse before, they will give you plenty of confidence and sympathetic guidance. The centre has been awarded the 'Ponies of Britain Purple Star for 1991', which is a very prestigious award indeed. Pony trekking is available and the Centre also organises unaccompanied children's hoidays, which is a wonderful idea for harassed parents in need of a break themselves! In addition to the Riding Centre, extremely comfortable Bed & Breakfast accommodation is available in the farmhouse.

One other notable 'feature' associated with the farm is a postcard! On sale throughout the county, it shows a goat peering out of one of the bedroom windows of the house. The photograph was taken before Janet took over the house and renovated it to its present superb condition, and it is entitled simply, 'At Home'. The benign looking creature seems just that - and we are sure you will feel the same way should you decide to stay here.

Alston & Killhope Riding Centre

At **Ireshopeburn**, between Wearhead and **St John's Chapel**, is the delightful little Weardale Museum, situated in the former minister's house next to an 18th century Methodist Chapel. The displays include a carefully re-created room in a typical Weardale lead-miner's cottage parlour, with furnishings and costumes in period and a special room dedicated to John Wesley.

St John's Chapel, Weardale

St John's Chapel was once the passenger terminus of the Weardale Railway and is still the home of annual Pennine sheep auctions which attract farmers from all over the North Pennines. This is the only village in Durham to boast a town hall, a small building in the classical style overlooking the village green.

From **Westgate** ran one of the most remarkable railway lines in the north of England - a mineral line built by the Weardale Iron Company along the high edge of the moors over to Rookhope, linked to Westgate and the valley bottom by the remarkable Scutterhill incline. It has survived as a moorland footpath, one of several which can be followed up valleys or moorland pocked with lead-mine workings and signs of former activity.

Westgate House is an elegant, mid-Victorian country house in Westgate and is the home of Stephanie and Hugh Williams. Between Easter and October they offer bed and breakfast accommodation with evening meal in four beautifully furnished rooms.

As you would expect in a house of this type, there are some very interesting features. Tucked away in the cellar is an authentic hand water-pump. More accessible is the original marble fireplace in the drawing-room, while a lovely 18th century frieze encircling the ceiling is painted in white and Wedgewood blue. Leaded lights in the French windows draw your eye to the views over the lawns in front of the house. Sharing these views is the dining room, furnished with Victorian antiques.

The large garden - one and a half acres in all - is beautiful and also secluded. How pleasant on a warm summer's day to emulate previous occupants with a leisurely game of croquet or a stroll to the edge of the garden along which flows the River Wear. Anglers can also take advantage of the fishing rights along this stretch of the river.

Westgate House

Lands Farm can be found just outside the village, in a perfectly tranquil setting where you can truly appreciate the meaning of the phrase 'peace and quiet'. The old stone-built farmhouse dates back mainly to the 18th century, though it may well be older in parts. As you sit in the large walled garden, all that can be heard is the singing of the birds and the gentle trickling of Swinhope Burn on the other side of the wall.

Mr and Mrs Reed have lived here for eight years now, although the farm has been in Mr Reed's family for 18 years. Rather than keeping this beautiful spot all to themselves, they have opened their doors to travellers who are looking for a place to relax in comfort for a night or two. Family and double rooms with en-suite are available, each room benefitting from central heating, television and tea and coffee making facilities. The attractive dining room is the setting for a full English or continental breakfast, which you can enjoy whilst looking out over the garden and planning your itinerary for the day.

Lands Farm

Rookhope is one of those hidden North Pennine valleys, mentioned in old Border ballads, which richly repay discovery and exploration. The remains of lead- and iron-mine activity, with some gauntly impressive monuments, now blend into quiet rural beauty. The burn (the Scottish word for a stream is commonly used in this part of Durham) shares the valley with the road which eventually climbs past the Rookhope Chimney, part of a lead-smelting mill where poisonous and metallic-rich fumes were refined in long flues, over Redburn Common to Allenheads in Northumberland.

Rookhope village has a history lost in antiquity, going back at least to Roman times. This history also has its macabre side, as reflected by the discovery some years ago, in a local quarry, of the Redburn Skulls - nine human skulls all carrying terrible teeth marks. Nobody has ever discovered how or why they came to be there, or who or what caused the teeth marks.

Rookhope was once the mining centre of Weardale and the public bar of the 17th century **Rookhope Inn** displays a number of photographs of the mine and village as it was at that time.

Set in dramatic and unspoilt hill country, this friendly pub offers comfortable three-bedroom accommodation in cosy surroundings and the undivided attention of the proprietors Mr and Mrs Lee.

Breakfast is, of course, served to residents, but for those just dropping in on their way through the dale, morning coffee, afternoon teas and good home-cooked bar meals are readily available, with the traditional roast joint on Sundays. Children are welcomed and small-portion meals are provided for them.

Although reputedly haunted by a 'grey lady' (records of which can be found in Durham University archives), Rookhope Inn remains deservedly popular with the local community, who fully appreciate the well-kept real ales and satisfying meals - ghost or no ghost!

Rookhope Inn

Stanhope, undoubtedly the capital of Upper Weardale, is a small town of great character and individuality, which still serves the surrounding villages as an important local centre for shops and supplies.

The stone cross in the Market Place is the only reminder of a once weekly market held in the town by virtue of a 1421 charter. The market continued until Victorian times.

The Bonny Moor Hen on Front Street is another old building which has enjoyed its share of history, for it became engulfed in the Battle of Stanhope. In these more peaceful times, it dispenses rest and refreshment to the local population and to travellers exploring the lush heart of Weardale.

The hotel has four-bedroom accommodation, two rooms en-suite, all of which have colour TV, tea and coffee making facilities and telephones. Children are gladly catered for and baby-listening services can be arranged on request. A cosy bar gives residents the opportunity to meet and chat to the 'regulars' with, perhaps, a game of pool.

The proprietors of this hotel also have three holiday cottages to let and will be pleased to receive enquiries about their availability.

The Bonny Moor Hen

Stanhope enjoyed its greatest period of prosperity in the 18th and 19th centuries when the lead and iron-stone industries were at their height. The town's buildings and architecture reflect this. In an attractive rural setting in the centre of the dale, with a choice of local walks, Stanhope, in its quiet way, is becoming a small tourist centre with pleasant shops and cafes. The town itself is well worth exploring on foot, and a useful 'walkabout' town trail is available locally or from Information Centres.

The most dominant building in the Market Square is Stanhope Castle, a rambling structure complete with mock-Gothic crenelated towers, galleries and battlements. The building is, in fact, an elaborate folly, dated 1798 and built on the site of a ruined medieval manor house. In 1875 it was enlarged to contain a private collection of mineral displays and stuffed birds for the entertainment of Victorian grouse-shooting parties.

Also here is the **Pack Horse Inn,** run by one of life's natural hosts, Charles Weeks. A fully qualified Master of Wines, he has served on the Queen Elizabeth II and together with his charming wife Sally, generates a really lively atmoshpere in this splendid pub. Situated in the heart of the village, the former coach house dates back to the 13th century, which is certainly one of the earliest we had come across in our travels. If you pop into the museum at Beamish, you may spot the Rob Roy Coach there on display - this was stabled at the Inn in former times.

The Pack Horse Inn

Other attractions at the Pack Horse include Charles' splendid array of miniatures that deck the walls, and on Saturday nights you can enjoy a good old sing-song with music provided by their talented accordionist! Sally is the guiding light behind the traditional English menu, which is always popular with visitors. Whatever your feelings about wines (and we love 'em!), Charles also stocks an excellent range of traditional beers and real ales. With bed and breakfast accommodation available and many plans for the future, the Pack Horse Inn is really going places. As the locals like to say, the Inn provides 'Good Food, Good Ale and Good Crack'. We wouldn't argue with that!

Stanhope Hall, above Stanhope Burn Bridge, is generally accepted to be one of the most impressive buildings in Weardale. This huge, fortified manor house was designed to repel Scottish raiders. It was the home of the famous Fetherstonehalgh family of Stanhope, who lived there from the mid-12th century until the last male heir was killed at the Battle of Blenheim in 1704. The hall itself is part medieval, part Elizabethan and part Jacobean. The outbuildings included a cornmill, a brew house and cattle yards.

The church of St Thomas, by the Market Square, has a Norman tower and some 13th century grave-covers to be found by the porch. In the churchyard you'll find a remarkable fossil tree stump that was discovered in 1962 in a local quarry.

One of the most important Bronze Age archaeological finds ever made in Britain was at Heathery Burn, a side valley off Stanhope Burn, when, in 1850, quarrymen cut through the floor of a cave to find a huge hoard of bronze and gold ornaments, amber necklaces, pottery, spearheads, animal bones and parts of chariots. The treasures are now kept in the British Museum.

Frosterley, further down the dale, has a name which again has hunting forest links and means 'forest lea'. When the Foresters' Arms was rebuilt in the last century, a hoard of medieval hunters' bows and arrows were found in the foundations of the old buildings.

The village is now more famous for its stone, including the celebrated Frosterley marble, a black, heavily-fossilised limestone which in former times was extensively used for rich decorative work and ornamentation on great public and private buildings throughout the north. The Chapel of the Nine Altars in Durham Cathedral makes extensive use of this stone, sometimes called 'Durham Marble'. There are huge limestone quarry remains to the south of the village, the stone having been taken out by rail over the last hundred years for use in the Teesside and Tyneside iron and steel furnaces.

Wolsingham, like Tow Law, has strong links with the iron and steel industries, the steelworks in the town being founded by one Charles Attwood who was one of the great pioneers in the manufacture of steel. The works once cast a variety of anchors and propellers for ships.

Wolsingham is also the home of England's oldest agricultural show, held in the market place on the first Saturday in September. Peel Cottage, on Front Street, was the town's first police station, named after Sir Robert Peel, whilst Whitfield Cottage, dated 1707, was once a packhorse inn.

The weekly 'bake' may be a thing of the past in most households, but to the lucky guests of Marjorie and John Anderson, the evocative smell of freshly baked bread is something to savour. The family run **Friarside Farm**, Wolsingham, a working farm producing much of the food required to feed bed and breakfast visitors.

Built in the 1600s, this grey stone farmhouse offers panoramic views of Weardale and has a comfortable and friendly atmosphere; the Visitors Book shows evidence of the esteem in which this establishment is held by both holidaymakers and guests from overseas. Apart from spacious accommodation in the farmhouse, there is a five berth self-catering caravan available in the grounds.

There is plenty to do in the area: swimming, bowls, pony-trekking, fishing and golf are all popular activities within easy reach and there is a leisure centre within eight miles of the farm.

Friarside Farm

Margaret and Hugh Tassell are the proud owners of Thistlewood Cottage, which sounds rather like something out of Beatrix Potter! They have only been in Wolsingham for a comparatively short time, and prior to this they owned a farm in Kent.

Thistlewood Hall lies on a secluded lane within walking distance of Wolsingham and all its amenities. The Cottage itself stands in the grounds of the Hall, an imposing Victorian house set in an acre of beautiful gardens, surrounded by attractive countryside.

The Cottage was originally a byre and has been refurbished to a very high standard. The accommodation comprises a modern kitchen fitted with every conceivable appliance, a superb living area, a fully fitted bathroom and two splendid bedrooms which can sleep four to five adults. The Cottage has its own private garden with patio, garden furniture and barbecue facilities, so you can really enjoy a secluded break here. One other feature of this lovely location is that the water for both the Hall and the Cottage comes from a private spring, which is absolutely pure and crystal clear.

Thistlewood Cottage

Tunstall Reservoir, north of Wolsingham, and reached by narrow lane or footpath, lies in a particularly interesting valley of ancient oak woods alongside Waskerley Beck. The reservoir was built in the mid-19th century, originally to provide lime-free water for the locomotives of The Stockton and Darlington Railway to prevent their boilers from scaling like a domestic kettle. It now forms part of a delightful area to stroll, picnic or go fishing.

A few miles south of Wolsingham lies **Hamsterley Forest**, one of the Forestry Commission's most attractive Forest Parks. This is a huge area - over 5,500 acres - of mature woodland, originally a private sporting estate, now managed for timber production and with 1,100 acres available for recreation with a choice of rides and walks. Today this firmly established area offers a wide range of activities for visitors, such as informal or guided walks, orienteering, horse-riding and cycling (cycles can be hired). There is a Visitor Centre with displays on forestry, wildlife and timber usage, and large, grassy areas make splendid picnic spots. The forest is easily accessible from coach and car parks and visitors are enthusiastically encouraged to enjoy the peace and quiet of this lovely place which is now a Forest Nature Reserve.

Surprisingly enough, the Forest is largely artificial and relatively recent in origin. Much of it covers areas once worked by the lead-mining industry. It was planted some 40 to 50 years ago with European larch, pine and Norway spruce but, in the clearings, several self-sown species have become established - ash, birch and oak among them, adding variety and colour. This is a good area to discover a range of wild flowers and, in the damper places, fungi. There are still red squirrels as well as roe-deer, badgers, adders and up to 40 species of birds including heron, woodcock, sparrowhawk, woodpeckers, fieldfare and goldfinch.

A farmstead in Weardale

North of Wolsingham and Stanhope, the moorland roads climb past Wolsingham Park Moor and Muggleswick Common, again part of the Prince Bishops' hunting domain, before descending into the Derwent

Valley, a tributary valley of the Tyne which forms part of the boundary between County Durham, Northumberland and Tyne and Wear.

Edmundbyers, just inside County Durham, is a typical, attractive moorland village whose church was founded in 1150. There is some fine interior woodwork here, and in the graveyard lie the remains of one of the last witches in the county. Edmundbyers makes an ideal starting point for an exploration of the Derwent Valley.

'Heatherside' is a charming cottage situated in the heart of the village. The bed and breakfast accommodation offered by Jill Bull is on the first floor of the cottage and comprises two double bedrooms, a bathroom and a sitting area which could also be used as an office. This would be an ideal place to take a breather while you plan your itinerary for the next day. The Punchbowl Inn can be found in the village and the Manor Restaurant is close by on the A68, so after enjoying a few drinks and a meal you can make your way back to Heatherside and sleep very soundly in the comfortable beds. Edmundbyers lies in an Area of Outstanding Natural Beauty, and there is plenty for the dedicated walker and nature lover to see and do. Not far from here is Derwent Reservoir, which is ideal for those who enjoy sailing and fishing. For further information, please write to Mrs Bull at 'Heatherside', Edmundbyers, Co. Durham DH8 9NL, or telephone (0207) 55674.

'Heatherside'

Blanchland Church

Tynedale

Hadrian's Wall

CHAPTER FIVE

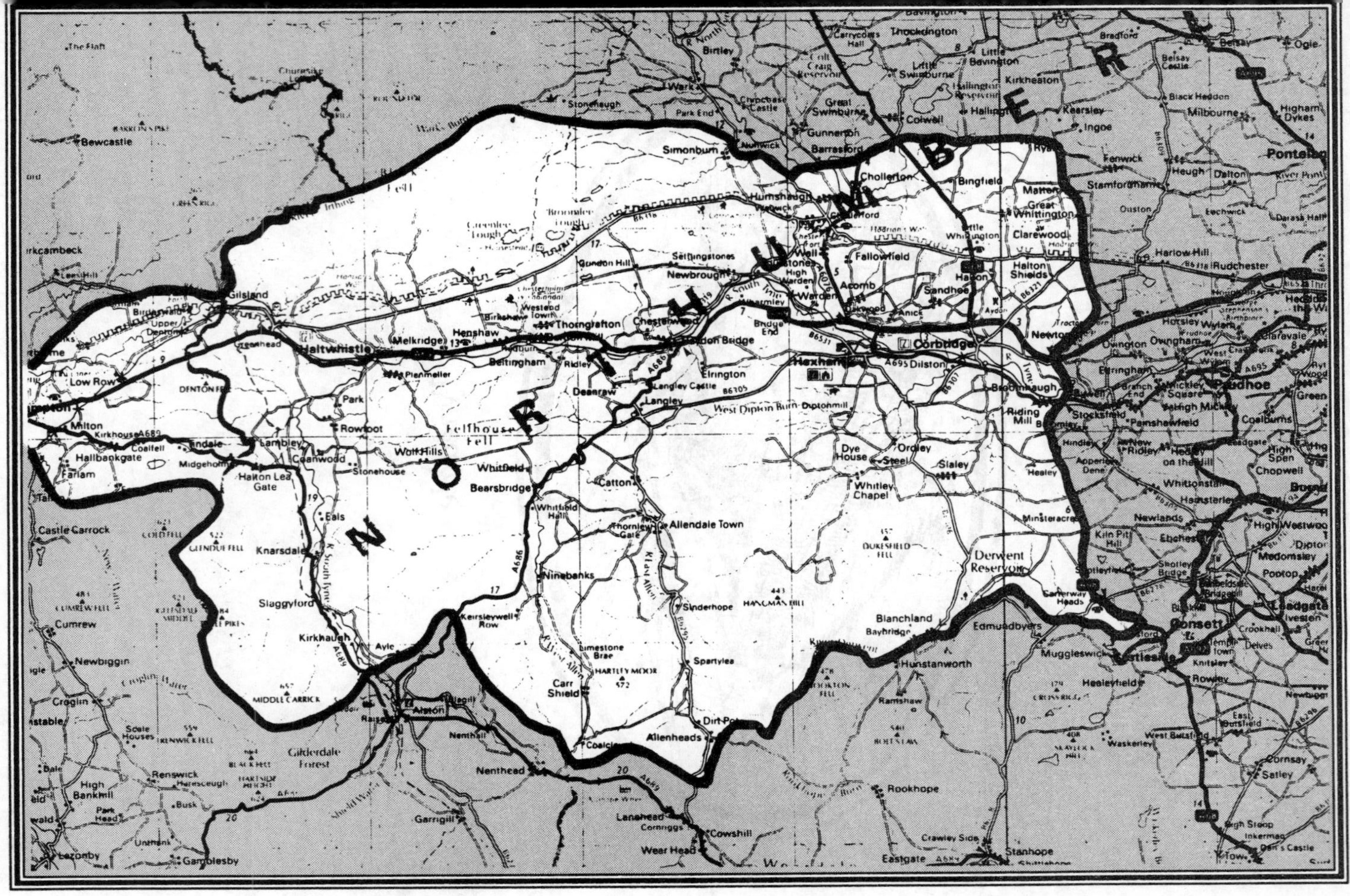

NORTHUMBERLAND
Gilsland
Haltwhistle
Melkridge
Henshaw
Bellingham
Thorngrafton
Chesterwood
Haydon Bridge
Newbrough
Simonburn
Humshaugh
Chollerton
Bingfield
Matfen
Great Whittington
Clarewood
Halton Shields
Fallowfield
Acomb
Sandhoe
Hexham
Corbridge
Dilston
Riding Mill
Broomhaugh
Newton
Stocksfield
Prudhoe
Ovingham
Langley
Langley Castle
Elrington
Deanraw
West Dipton Burn
Felthouse Fell
Wolf Hills
Whitfield
Bearsbridge
Catton
Allendale Town
Ninebanks
Sinderhope
Spartylea
Allenheads
Carr Shield
Limestone Brae
Hartley Moor
Dye House
Steel
Ordley
Slaley
Whitley Chapel
Derwent Reservoir
Blanchland
Edmundbyers
Hunstanworth
Rookhope
Stanhope
Eastgate
Wear Head
Cowshill
Nenthead
Alston
Garrigill
Kirkhaugh
Slaggyford
Knarsdale
Eals
Lambley
Coanwood
Halton Lea Gate
Rowfoot
Park
Low Row
Milton
Hallbankgate
Farlam
Castle Carrock
Cumrew
Newbiggin
Croglin
Renwick
Gilderdale Forest
Bewcastle
Simonburn
Wark
Birtley
Barrasford
Gunnerton
Colwell
Kirkheaton
Belsay
Ponteland
Stamfordham
Fenwick
Ingoe
Harlow Hill
Rudchester
Horsley
Consett
Castleside
Muggleswick
Healeyfield
Shotley Bridge
Satley
Cornsay
Medomsley
Chopwell
Hamsterley
Newlands

Chapter Five - Map Reference Guide
Tynedale

Aydon Grange - Corbridge

New Mills Trout Farm - Brampton

Hotspur Hotel - Allendale Town

Rye Hill Farm - Slaley

The Beaumont Hotel - Hexham

Riverside Leisure - Hexham

Burnt Walls - Greenhead

Oaky Knowe Farm - Haltwhistle

Goodies at Gresham Lodge - Corbridge

Vallum Lodge Hotel - Twice Brewed

Crowberry Hall - Allendale

The White Lion Hotel - Brampton

Holmehead Farm Guest House - Greenhead

Vicar's Pele, Corbridge

CHAPTER FIVE

Tynedale

The River Tyne, one of the loveliest rivers of England's North Country, is essentially a river of the Pennines and the Cheviot Hills, but it has a split personality. The South Tyne rises on the shoulders of Cross Fell, in Cumbria, before winding its way northwards through Alston and the Upper Tyne valley, past Slaggyford and Lambley, to Haltwhistle. From here it begins its long journey eastwards to Newcastle and the coast. The North Tyne begins life as tiny moorland burns, high up on the fellsides of the Cheviots, before joining the South Tyne west of Hexham to become a single river.

Tynedale itself - or more accurately, the South Tyne Valley - forms a great natural pass across the Pennines. To the north lies the Northumberland National Park; to the south is Allendale, one of the most spectacularly beautiful of the Tyne's tributaries. The main valley carries river, railway and the trunk-road between Newcastle and Carlisle, but more impressive than any of these is the North of England's greatest single man-made monument - Hadrian's Wall.

Discovering the wall is still a thrilling experience which inspires a sense of wonder at being at the northern boundary of a mighty empire which stretched from Egypt and North Africa to these cool, green hills. The wall, seven feet wide and built of rough, weatherworn stones, was built to keep wild Pictish tribesmen at bay.

The wall and its series of regular turrets, small milecastles, great defensive ditch, or Vallum, to the rear and major forts, were served by excellent roads at frequent strategic intervals. How it came to be built along the perimeter of this northern valley is a complex piece of history and engineering, reflecting changing fortunes of the mighty Roman legions under General Julius Agricola and his successors. It was left to the Emperor Hadrian, on a visit to Britain in 122AD, to take the decision to cut the empire's losses with an impregnable wall from the Tyne to the Solway, north of the old Roman road known as Stanegate.

Much of this immense work was done in the four short years between 122AD and 126AD. The wall was virtually abandoned between 140AD and 166AD when the Romans believed they had taken control of Southern Scotland, and the Antonine Wall was built between the Forth and the Clyde to hold back the ferocious Highlanders. When this was proved inadequate to restrain the Picts, the Roman frontier returned to Tynedale and Hadrian's Wall was further reinforced. It was then linked to good roads such as The Maiden Way and Dere Street from the south, which enabled troop reinforcements to be rushed to weak points along the defences.

The finest section of the wall for the present day visitor lies between Chollerford and Gilsland, where it runs close to the B6318, the so-called Military Road, built by General Wade to help defeat the Jacobites in the 18th century. But the best preserved and undoubtedly the most impressive sections of all - inevitably the most photographed - lie near Housesteads, north of Bardon Mill. Here there is a superbly situated fort, overlooking Greenlee and Broomlee Loughs, which contains the only visible example of a Roman hospital. Near by runs a magnificent section of extremely well-preserved wall along a high ridge of dark Whin Sill rock, rising to its highest point at Winshields, some 1,200ft above sea level. This is a magnifient viewpoint, with the brooding waters of Crag Lough below. Excellent access can be made to this part of the wall near the evocatively named hamlet of Twice Brewed, through the centre of which the Vallum runs, past Peel Crag and Steel Rigg.

At **Twice Brewed**, the **Vallum Lodge Hotel** stands on the edge of Northumberland National Park within sight of Hadrian's Wall and is run by Jack and Christine Wright, who have created that atmosphere of friendliness and hospitality so characteristic of a small hotel.

In the evenings, the bar invites reminiscences of the day's pursuits in this peaceful and unspoilt countryside. Jack, a fisherman himself, enjoys sharing his broad knowledge of local wildlife and habitat with guests.

Christine's speciality is the evening cuisine, served in the small and cosy restaurant. From the soup course onwards everything is freshly prepared and she has every reason to be proud ofher selection ofhome-cooked dishes.

Adjacent to the hotel is a small shop displaying work by local craftsmen and artists. Woodcrafts are especially prominent and Jack offers a personal framing service for prints and photographs to individual order.

Vallum Lodge Hotel

About two miles due south-west, close to the village of **Once Brewed** (which, like Twice Brewed, takes its name from an old carriers' inn), is Vindolanda Fort and Roman Museum where there are the remains of no less than eight successive forts built to house troops. There is also a full-scale replica of a section of the wall and actual Roman writing implements, textiles, leather and wooden objects. At Greenhead there is a Roman Army Museum, and another impressive Fort and Museum can be visited at Chesters, just west of Chollerford. Several of the smaller structures, such as milecastles and turrets, can be visited and it is also possible to walk on, or close to, much of the wall.

The best section for walking, however (pending completion of the proposed Hadrian's Walk National Trail in the mid 1990s), is the 12-mile stretch between Sewingshields, north of Haydon Bridge, and Greenhead. During the summer months a special Roman Wall Bus Service links sites of interest between Bardon Mill and Hexham railway stations.

Burnt Walls is a typical Northumbrian stone farmhouse, enlarged by its present owners, Peter and Geraldine Walker, to offer comfortable home from home accommodation in traditional surroundings.

This attractive farmhouse is set back from the B6318 between

Greenhead and **Gilsland**, which are both just west of Haltwhistle on the main A69 road. Its rural location just outside the Northumberland National Park within half a mile of Hadrian's Wall and the Pennine Way makes it an ideal base for touring this fascinating countryside.

Although Burnt Walls is not a working farm, Geraldine has just started breeding Cashmere goats and the rarer Golden Guernsey goat. The house itself - partially built with stone taken from Hadrian's Wall - stands in over one acre of grounds with extensive views over open countryside.

Visitors are assured of an interesting stay in this cosy house, with its open fire, full central heating and colour TV. Being a professional genealogist, Geraldine is happy to offer guests the benefit of her expertise in tracing family histories. There are

three guest bedrooms in all, one of which is a family room and can be booked at reduced rates.

Non-smokers are preferred at Burnt Walls, and those who decide to avail themselves of Geraldine's hospitality will find that she offers full English breakfast, and evening meals by arrangement. Vegetarians can also be catered for. All meals are home cooked and local produce is used whenever possible. If you're intending to get out and about for the day, a lunch can be packed for you.

Burnt Walls

Burnt Walls is open from February to November and offers peace and tranquillity in this exciting and interesting part of the world. All those who can fully appreciate what is on offer here are assured of a warm welcome.

You will be surrounded by some fascinating bird and animal wildlife as well as legendary castles and villages - visit Gilsland where Sir Walter Scott proposed to his wife at what is now known as the Popping Stone.

Peter and Geraldine know the local area and its history well - we are sure you will find what they have to say truly fascinating and that you will thank us for introducing you to such a hospitable and exciting destination.

Slightly north of Greenhead, astride Hadrian's Wall, is **Holmehead Farm Guest House.** This lovely farmhouse is over 150 years old and is also built with stone taken from the historic Wall itself. The owners, Pauline and Brian Staff, are understandably proud of its renovation and modernisation.

There are three twin-bedded rooms and one family room, but there is also a self-catering flat within the farmhouse which offers all the facilities guests need to make their stay a comfortable and relaxing one. Disabled visitors can enjoy unhindered access into and around the flat.

Mr and Mrs Staff claim to offer their guests the longest breakfast menu in the world - and both breakfast and dinner are made from the finest local produce.

Holmehead Farm Guest House

You can easily spend an excellent week's holiday simply walking by the wall between the Tyne and the Solway and visiting its many remarkable and evocative sites, but there is even more to Tynedale than the wall.

Alston, reputed to be the highest market town in England, happens to be in Cumbria, but it is on the Tyne and is a natural focal point for Upper Tynedale. The South Tyne Railway - a charming, narrow-gauge, steam-line which has some superb steam locomotives from both Britain and Eastern Europe - runs from Alston, across the boundary into Northumberland to its first new station, Gilderdale.

The line is already being extended towards **Slaggyford** and may eventually reach **Lambley** where a magnificent, but unsafe, viaduct will impede its progress along the line of the original standard-gauge railway to **Haltwhistle**. In the meantime, the journey along the main A689 by bus or car is a very acceptable alternative, a deep gorge with river, railway and road sharing the narrow valley between the bare hills; high fells such as Snope Common, Black Hill and Glendue Fell. The Pennine Way also goes along the valley, at one point taking the line of the Maiden Way, a Roman Road, which follows the shoulder of the hillside across to Greenhead and Hadrian's Wall. At Whitley Castle, about half a mile south of Kirkhaugh, are the foundations of a Roman fort on the Maiden Way.

Rather better preserved is Featherstone Castle, not open to the public but an impressive castellated house, rebuilt in high Victorian style, though with genuine 13th century fragments incorporated into its western end. Between 1945-48, it was a Prisoner of War Camp for German officers, one of whom, Captain Herbert Sulzbach OBE, their interpreter, dedicated himself to the cause of post-war Anglo-German reconciliation.

New Mills Trout Farm

New Mills Trout Farm, on the A69 east of **Brampton**, is an interesting and enjoyable place to spend a day and offers something for all the family.

Owned by Bill and Jay Gray, New Mills has been operating since May 1982 and produces high-quality, pink-fleshed rainbow-trout mainly for the table. The farm is situated on Quarry Beck and three million gallons of water pass through the complex each day.

Visitors can either buy the produce from the farm shop after choosing exactly the size required (anything from 8oz to 10lbs) or spend the day fishing the lake; there is a limit of a four-fish catch for adults, two for children. Children will also, no doubt, enjoy feeding the fish themselves from floating walkways; special high-protein pellets are available from the farm shop for this purpose. There is reasonable access to the lakeside for disabled people in wheelchairs and the owners will offer every assistance.

Overlooking the trout farm is **The Olde Granary**, a 16th century building now delightfully refurbished as a licensed restaurant and resplendent with polished, pine tables. Here Shona Coulthard, the daughter of Bill and Jay Gray, personally prepares and cooks delicious, light lunches and sumptuous afternoon teas; the scones, tea-breads, biscuits and cakes really are home-made. The Olde Granary also serves morning coffee, and freshly-made sandwiches are available throughout the day.

The Olde Granary

The ancient market town of Brampton was the headquarters of Bonnie Prince Charlie in his seige of Carlisle in 1745. There is a plaque to commemorate this on a black-and-white building in High Cross Street. After the suppression by the Duke of Cumberland of the Jacobite rebellion, six local supporters were hanged.

The White Lion Hotel in High Cross Street, run by Sarah and James Johnson, provides a warm family welcome to all who stay at this charming country hotel, where old beams and real log fires add to the cosy atmosphere.

Centrally placed, this is a very convenient hotel from which to see Brampton. Good home-cooking is the order of the day at the White Lion, with special daily dishes an added attraction to the main menu.

The White Lion Hotel

The octagonal Moot Hall in the market place, with its handsome clock-tower, is Brampton's most striking building. The present Hall was built in 1817 by Lord Carlisle, but there has been a Moot Hall since 1648. Originally, the lower part was open, but it was enclosed in 1896. The iron stocks at the foot of a double flight of external stairs were last used in 1836. Just off the market square is St Martin's Church, which was rebuilt in 1878. It was designed by Philip Webb, a member of the pre-Raphaelite Brotherhood, who requested that stained glass should be installed. Climb up to the wooded mound for a magnificent view of the Solway plain and the distinctive Scottish mountains on the Galloway coast.

The South Tyne turns east just below the watershed with the River Irthing. Here the little Tipall Burn winds east into Northumberland from the Cumbrian border to **Greenhead**, an attractive village with a fine Victorian church. Here and at nearby Gilsland (which is actually divided by the Roman wall) river, road, railway and wall seem to come together. Thirwall Castle, to the north of Greenhead and guarding the pass at this point, was built, like so much else in this part of Tynedale, of stone taken from the wall.

Haltwhistle, a small town with an open feel to it, is host to the South Tyne Annual Agricultural Show and has regular cattle and sheep markets. Its name owes nothing to the railway but comes from the Norman-Saxon word 'haut wiscle', meaning 'junction of streams by a hill'. It is difficult to imagine that this pleasant little town with its grey terraces was once a mining area, but local industries remain. The church of the Holy Cross, behind the Market Place, goes back to the 13th century and is said to be on the site of a 12th century church founded by William the Lion, King of Scotland.

Near by, we were delighted to discover **Oaky Knowe Farm**. Owners Pat and Maurice Murray are a cheerful, friendly couple who always make everyone welcome. They have owned and run the 300-acre farm for 18 years, and being situated within easy reach of National Trust land, the views are truly magnificent. Guests are encouraged to explore the full extent of the farm land so they can get a real flavour of this beautiful countryside. This is very much a home from home, and the two family rooms are most comfortable. Pat cooks all the meals and also eats with her guests, which is rather nice as you feel like one of the family. Also part of the team is Ringo the Jack Russell, a friendly little chap who makes a point of greeting people with much wagging of his tail. Although you are guaranteed all the peace and quiet you could wish for here, Oakley Knowe is set back less than a mile from the main A69, making it an ideal base from which to tour further afield.

Oaky Knowe Farm

Between Haltwhistle, Bardon Mill and Haydon Bridge lies a particularly attractive section of Tynedale, with scattered woodlands giving the valley a gentler feel. There are some excellent opportunities for walking, with attractive footpaths along and around the valley, perhaps taking advantage of the railway stations on the Tyne Valley railway line. Bardon Mill owes its name to a former woollen mill which is now a pottery turning out both utilitarian drain-pipes and handsome, terracotta plan-pots. Haydon Bridge, as its name implies, is an ancient crossing point of the Tyne, much fought over by the English and Scots. The old bridge remains, the present one, dating from 1773, being rebuilt after the great Tyne Flood, though three arches on the south of the bridge were replaced in the 19th century.

Between Bardon Mill and Haydon Bridge lies the confluence with the River Allen, which, like the Tyne, soon splits into two - the East Allen and West Allen.

Allendale really is a hidden jewel. Allen Banks, as the lower part of the valley is known, is a deeply wooded limestone valley, rich in natural beauty, now owned by the National Trust. You can park at the picnic site close to the disused Plankey Mill, (reached by lane from the main A686 Alston road) and take a choice of riverside walks. Crossing the river by a suspension bridge, the path goes through a woodland of pine, beech, oak, birch, ash and elder, past Raven Crag, an outcrop of limestone from where the ravens still fly with raucous voices. This is an area particularly rich in wild flowers, ferns, mosses and rhododendrons. Nearby Ridley Hall, now a private school, was the seat of the Ridley family, the most celebrated of whom was Bishop Nicholas Ridley (1500-55), burnt at the stake by Queen Mary I. The hamlet of Beltingham has stone-roofed 18th century cottages around a little green.

The main route into Allendale from Hexham is the A686 to Alston which follows the West Allen past Langley Castle, a massive keep built around 1350 by Sir Thomas de Lucy to keep out the Scots. It was restored in the 1890s by a local historian, C.J. Bates. From here, the road follows a narrow pass of quite breathtaking beauty, curving around a hairpin bend to cross the richly wooded gorge of the Allen itself. Here the river divides into its twin tributaries, before climbing over the moors past Willyshaw Rigg to descend into Alston.

If you have ever wanted to try your hand at craftwork but have found the equipment too expensive or have been put off by the thought that it just may be too difficult for you, think again! At **Crowberry Hall,** John and Isabel Wentzel offers an opportunity for beginners to try their hand at a large selection of creative activities from leatherwork to lacemaking, corn dollies to quilting, patchwork to pressed flowers, water colours to weaving, and whittling, in the peaceful setting of an Area of Outstanding Natural Beauty.

Residential students receive 15 hours of basic tuition and use of equipment with five nights bed and breakfast, mid-day snack and evening meal. Isabel enjoys cooking and aims to offer quality and choice, so guests are involved in discussions on the day's menu which is largely home-prepared, including the bread and preserves.

Though the courses, which are also open to non-residents, take place in spring and autumn, Crowberry Hall is open all year round and this is an ideal place for a restful holiday in superb historic countryside.

Crowberry Hall

Allendale Town lies on the East Allen River and is reached by the B6303 from Langley or Hexham. Like Alston, this village was once an important centre of the North Pennine lead-mining industry. It retains attractive houses from prosperous times and a suprisingly large number of existing or former inns around the Market Square. A sundial in the churchyard records the fact that the village lies at latitude 54' 60", making it exactly the mid point between Beachy Head in Sussex and Cape Wrath in Scotland. This allows the town to claim to be at the very centre of Britain.

The Hotspur Hotel is a substantial, stone building just off the market square in Allendale. The name 'Hotspur' is historically significant, of course, as it recalls the ancient Percy family who were Dukes of Northumberland. Shakespeare immortalised their most renowned member, 'Harry Hotspur', in 'Henry IV, Part 1'.

On a somewhat different note, the hotel itself was affectionately remembered by Catherine Cookson when she based 'Doctor Arnison's' surgery on it in her novels.

The real history of this hotel begins in 1806; this date, as well as 1883, when it was rebuilt, is etched in the stone lintel in what is now the games room. It is run by sisters, Sandra and Florence, local people who are known for their country, farmhouse-style of cooking. Their reputation for excellent home-cooking attracts visitors from far afield, particularly for Sunday lunch. Guests who stay here find it a comfortable and relaxing base from which to explore the unspoilt countryside. The bedrooms are spacious, some are en-suite, and the service is typified by the willingness to collect guests arriving at the local station.

Hotspur Hotel

Allenheads, higher up the twisting valley, also has lead-mining connections, with its scatter of stone miners' cottages and an irregular village square with pub and chapel in a lovely setting. This is also a centre for fine, upland rambles through the surrounding hills, which still retain many signs of the former industrial activity.

From here the main road climbs over Burtree Fell into Weardale, with wild moorland roads branching across to Rookhope or Nenthead.

Returning to the main Tyne valley, **Hexham**, built on a terrace overlooking the river, is the capital and administrative centre of Tynedale, and this busy little town, so rich in Tynedale character, should not be missed. The great Abbey goes back to 674AD, at which time it was reputed to be the 'largest and most magnificent church this side of the Alps'. Though it may now have a few rivals for such a title, the present building is still on a magnificent scale, with many Saxon remains from the original church. These include the Crypt, said to be the finest of its period in existence, and the 1,300-year-old St Wilfrid's Chair or Frith Stool. There is also some wonderful late-medieval architecture, mainly from the 12th and 13th centuries, which later restoration has certainly not diminished. Not only is there a rich heritage of carved stone-work, but Hexham is also famous for its woodcarving. The early 16th century rood screen has been described as the best in any monastic church in Britain.

Hexham Abbey

There is also much more to see in Hexham. The Tourist Information Centre, in the Market Place, uses the Manor Office, a building that dates back to 1330. The Middle March Centre for Border History is located in the 14th century Manor House and tells, in a vivid way, the story of the border struggles between the two nation states. The territory was hotly disputed, and for many centuries was virtually without rule of law, subject to the activities of the notorious 'Reivers' - cattle rustlers and thieves who took advantage of the disputed border lands. The powerful Wardens, or Lords of the Marches - themselves warlords of pitiless ferocity - were given almost complete authority by the King to control the 'Reivers' and anyone else who crossed their path. This was the period of the great medieval Border Ballads, violent and colourful tales of love, death, heroism and betrayal which have found an enduring place in literature, and which came from this region.

The town has kept much of its character, with winding lanes and passageways, some delightful shops and a Tuesday market. There are some attractive 18th and 19th century houses, handsome terraces, delightful gardens around the priory, and several attractive areas of open space. These include the area around The Seal, and there are particularly good views, from several points in the town, across the Tyne valley.

Adjacent to and overlooking the abbey and gardens is the **Beaumont Hotel,** an imposing stone building erected at the turn of the century. Previously a temperance establishment called the Abbey Hotel, the building was re-named in 1964 when the temperance connection was discontinued.

Run by Martin and Linda Owen, these spacious premises offer 23-bedroom accommodation in an ideal location just off the main shopping area and are perfectly situated as a base from which to explore ancient Northumbria.

The Beaumont Hotel

The hotel's Park Restaurant provides table d'hote and a la carte menus of intriguing complexity - so much to choose from - but dishes such as Snails and Wild Mushrooms sauteed in garlic and red wine and Boned and Shallow Fried Whole Dover Sole in lobster and oyster sauce must surely give the reader some idea of the expertise of the Beaumont's chefs.

Aperitifs can be enjoyed in the cocktail bar; residents may obtain morning coffee or afternoon tea here during the day.

The Beaumont has facilities for small private functions or conferences in the Abbey Suite, while larger occasions, such as dinner dances or wedding receptions, are held in the elegant ballroom.

Riverside Leisure on Tyne Green offers guests accommodation in luxury holiday homes in one of the best Country Garden parks we have ever seen. The setting is lovely, and if you travel in your own camper you will find excellent facilities laid on. Guests can choose from several styles to suit their pocket and the pitches and self-catering holiday units are spotlessly maintained.

Riverside Leisure

One of the biggest attractions of this holiday park is the amount of leisure activities you can enjoy. The list is almost endless and when you look at the location of the park, you realise that you can get to the Roman Wall and all the noted local beauty spots and attractions in a very short time. Near by there is fishing, golfing, pony trekking, cycling, play areas, swimming, and canoeing - or you can simply relax. In this wooded garden park wildlife abounds and the most likely disturbance will be the sound of the river or the chimes of the Abbey clock. Don't forget to take your camera. Owner Mr Pickering quite candidly states, 'We're not the biggest Park in the North. Neither do we want to be.' We couldn't agree more - it is far better to ensure that your guests feel relaxed and benefit from the peace and fine views than to simply cater for greater numbers.

Chollerford, some five miles north of Hexham along the valley, enjoys an exceptionally fine setting, including a delightful area of parkland which includes part of the wall. This celebrated Roman Fort, 'Chesters', covers five-and-three-quarter acres and was large enough to accommodate a full cavalry regiment. The handsome bridge across the river is 100 yards long and was built in 1775.

Corbridge, four miles down river from Hexham but on the opposite bank of the Tyne, is another ancient market town; it was, for a time, the actual capital of the ancient Kingdom of Northumbria and it was here, in 796AD, that King Ethelred of Northumbria was murdered. This charming place still retains relics of its former importance as a strategic crossing of the river, including two fortified medieval towers, Low Hall and the Vicar's Pele, an impressive 17th century bridge, and St Andrews, one of the oldest churches in Northumbria.

There is also narrow Middle Street with its superb range of high quality shops, and the interesting nooks and crannies in the town - all very much worth exploring. Should you care to visit the Roman site of Corstopitum, or walk along part of Hadrian's Wall, then Corbridge is the perfect place to stop on your journey.

Roman columns at Corstopitum

Gresham House in Watling Street is an interesting and beautiful resting place in the town. The Victorian House dominates Watling Street, and if you ask the owner, Ron Learmouth, about its own history, he will be delighted to tell you while you enjoy something delicious to eat and drink in the Garden Room. This is a licensed restaurant and tearoom on the far side of the house, with wonderful views from the two bay windows over the Tyne Valley to Hexham.

This light and elegant room is a perfect setting for homemade food of high quality, and when you have finished your meal, there are two shops for you to visit in the adjoining rooms on the ground floor. **Goodies** is a most fascinating Embroidery and Tapestry shop with all manner of threads, fabrics, canvasses, kits and accessories for the needleworker, together with a large range of other unusual gift items for the person who is difficult to please. Gresham House Antiques is a treasure trove of Georgian and Victorian furniture, as well as small pieces of glass, china and silver, and other old and valuable items from bygone ages. Ron specialises in light fittings, and there are always oil lamps and unusual lights amongst the larger items.

If you can prise yourself away from the shops, there are excellent walks through and beside the town, either into the countryside or along the river. Corbridge is a 'must' for the visitor to Northumberland.

Goodies at Gresham Lodge

At Aydon Castle, three miles along the B6321 from Corbridge, is a superb example of a Northumbrian fortified manor house or small castle, the fortification being necessary in this region during the turbulent Middle Ages to keep the 'Reivers' at bay. It is now open to the public.

Close by, the entrance to **Aydon Grange** is clearly indicated. Set in three acres, this country manor house enjoys open views across the Tyne valley; and the owners, Angela and Derek Straker, give their bed and breakfast guests a family welcome, as this is very much their home.

In the tastefully furnished dining room there is ample space to enjoy the traditional sideboard English breakfast and also, in the evenings, the 'candlelit dinner' (to be ordered in advance) which is an elegant treat.

Self-catering holidays are offered at the attractive cottage adorned with climbing roses and clematis, at the entrance to the grounds. Aydon Grange Cottage is single-storeyed and has its own private garden shaded by lovely mature trees. Furnished to a high standard, it has three large bedrooms and a comfortable sitting room with an open fire. The secluded, hard tennis-court, which belongs to the main house, can also be used by guests staying here.

The Strakers can provide a great deal of local information about the many attractions and activities in the area, together with packed lunches if required.

Highly commended by the English Tourist Board, Aydon Grange has been awarded three crowns.

Aydon Grange

There is an area of little known, but charming, countryside south of Corbridge; undulating, and bounded on one side by the steep, little valley of Devil's Water and on the other by the main A68. Dominated by two large areas of afforestation, Dipton Wood and Slaley Forest, this area is penetrated by a network of narrow lanes and moorland tracks. Several of these lead across Blanchland Moor to the remote village of **Blanchland**, one of the loveliest in Northumberland, in a matchless setting of heather moorland, its high river-bridge crossing into County Durham. This was originally a monastic settlement, and the outline of the village reflects the layout of the 12th century Premonstratensian Abbey. A section of the walls of the 13th century guest-house form part of the village inn. The 15th century gate-house and the 13th century abbey church, still in use as the parish church, survive.

A holiday of a particularly high standard can be enjoyed at **Rye Hill Farm, Slaley**. Occupying three sides of a courtyard, the 300-year-old farmhouse and converted stone byres provide extremely comfortable, seven bedroom, bed and breakfast accommodation and a high quality self-catering cottage for six to eight people. All the ground floor is suitable for the disabled. There is also a games room for use by all.

Rye Hill Farm

Under the friendly and helpful guidance of the owner-manager, Elizabeth Courage and her family, visitors to Rye Hill Farm are assured of a very pleasant and relaxing stay in this lovely part of Tynedale. There are marvellous views of the surrounding peaceful countryside.

Mrs Courage, a good country cook, caters for breakfasts and optional evening meals, and has never knowingly bought a pot of jam! Nearly everything is home-made. There is also a table license. Well-mannered children and pets are most welcome.

Rye Hill is a working farm set in 30 acres of land just off the B6306 Blanchland to Hexham road. The farm has sheep, goats, pigs, poultry and ponies and gives the visitor - and especially, perhaps, the children - an opportunity to sample real farm life and even to try milking the goats.

Blanchland lies at the head of Derwent Reservoir, now very much a place for recreation and nature conservation, a favourite place for birdwatchers with car parks on both the Northumberland and the Durham banks. At Pow Hill there is a small country park with fine views over the reservoir.

It is worth making the journey further east, along the A695 towards the Tyne and Wear boundary, to **Prudhoe** to enjoy the massive medieval castle whose walls are 26ft high and over five feet thick. Once a seat of the Percy family, Earls of Northumberland, and a great bastion against invasion by the Scots, it is now owned and managed by English Heritage, and is in an exceptionally good state of preservation.

Only three miles away, just east of **Wylam,** is a very different kind of monument - the humble cottage, now a small museum by a former railway track, where George Stephenson was born in 1781 and lived until the age of eight. A wooden tramway ran past the cottage, carrying trains of coal trucks from Wylam Colliery to Lemington where the coal was loaded onto Tyne barges. Stephenson's first duties in life included ensuring that his young brothers and sisters were not run over by the horse-drawn waggons; later he was allowed to walk along the tramway to the colliery engine-house where his father worked.

Tyneside

Washington Old Hall

CHAPTER SIX

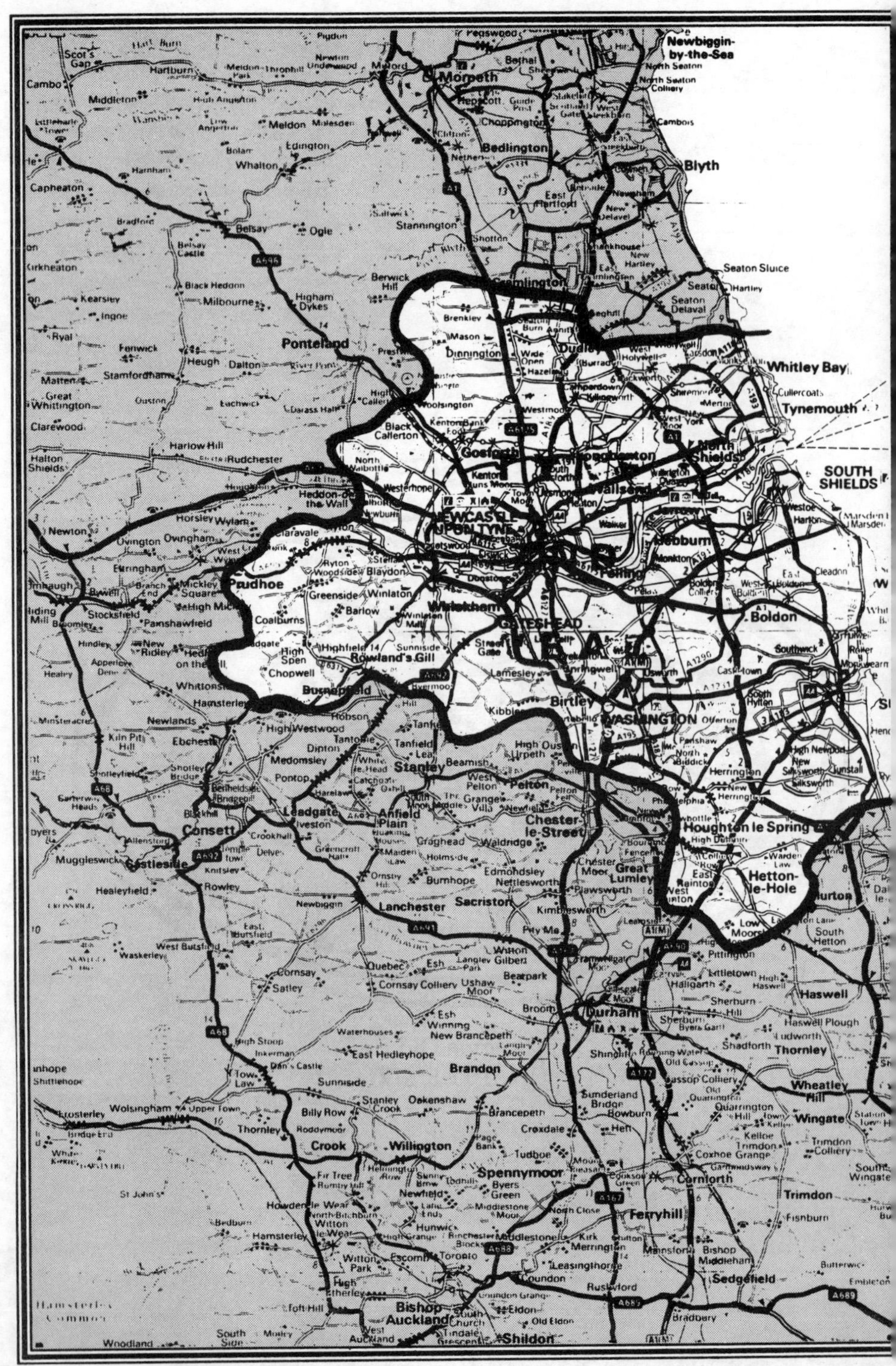

Newbiggin-by-the-Sea
North Seaton
North Seaton Colliery
Scot's Gap
Hartburn
Cambo
Middleton
Meldon
Whalton
Morpeth
Bedlington
Choppington
Cambois
Blyth
Capheaton
Belsay
Ogle
Stannington
Kirkheaton
Belsay Castle
Black Heddon
Kearsley
Milbourne
Ingoe
Higham Dykes
Berwick Hill
Ryal
Fenwick
Heugh
Dalton
Ponteland
Stamfordham
Matten
Great Whittington
Clarewood
Harlow Hill
Rudchester
Halton Shields
Seaton Sluice
Seaton Delaval
Cramlington
Dudley
Brenkley
Dinnington
Wide Open
Whitley Bay
Cullercoats
Tynemouth
North Shields
SOUTH SHIELDS
Black Callerton
Gosforth
Kenton
Wallsend
Heddon-on-the-Wall
Horsley
Wylam
Newton
Ovington
Ovingham
NEWCASTLE UPON TYNE
Hebburn
Jarrow
Felling
Prudhoe
Ryton
Blaydon
Winlaton
Greenside
Barlow
Whickham
Coalburns
GATESHEAD
Boldon
Cleadon
Westoe
Harton
High Spen
Chopwell
Rowland's Gill
Burnopfield
Sunniside
Lamesley
Birtley
WASHINGTON
Usworth
Southwick
Castletown
Stocksfield
Bywell
Mickley Square
Riding Mill
Hindley
New Ridley
Whittonstall
Hamsterley
Newlands
Ebchester
Hobson
High Westwood
Tanfield
Stanley
Dipton
Medomsley
Beamish
Pelton
Shotley Bridge
Consett
Leadgate
Annfield Plain
Chester-le-Street
Castleside
Muggleswick
Lanchester
Sacriston
Great Lumley
Houghton le Spring
Hetton-le-Hole
Herrington
Pittington
Haswell
Durham
Esh Winning
Brandon
Shadforth
Thornley
Wheatley Hill
Wingate
Tow Law
Wolsingham
Frosterley
Crook
Willington
Spennymoor
Ferryhill
Cornforth
Trimdon
Sedgefield
Bishop Auckland
Shildon
West Auckland
Woodland
Hamsterley Common

Chapter Six - Map Reference Guide
Tyneside

The Wheatsheaf Hotel - Woolsington

The Holiday Inn - Seaton Burn

Gateshead Parks - Gateshead

The Bridge End Inn - Ovingham

Dial Cottage, Killingworth

CHAPTER SIX

Tyneside

Where the rivers Tyne and Wear come down from the Pennines, crossing the narrow coastal plain to meet the North Sea, densely populated towns and cities have grown, over centuries, around their broad estuaries; towns that have relied on the two great rivers for the transport of goods by both river and sea, allowing their industries, particularly coal-mining and shipbuilding, to flourish.

But this great industrial conurbation, now combined into the Metropolitan County of Tyne and Wear, has a rich heritage of its own and some surprises.

As it leaves the Pennines, Weardale becomes Wearside - far less widely celebrated outside the region than its neighbour to the north, Tyneside, yet having a special character of its own.

The Bridge End Inn, at **Ovingham**, is named after an old pack-horse bridge over a burn which runs into the Tyne about half a mile away. Local history suggests it was an old coaching inn, and its age (300 years old) and character would seem to confirm this.

The inn is open all day from 11am to 11pm and visitors can enjoy a good bar meal in the comfortable and pleasant surroundings of the olde worlde bar and cottage-style lounge.

Quite recently, accommodation has opened for those wishing to stay overnight. Newly built on the site of the old stables, there are several single and double rooms, decorated with traditional furnishings.

Wearside also enjoys a piece of rather special North Country mythology, that of the 'Lambton Worm'.

This medieval legend, celebrated in ballad, tells of a young knight from a local noble family, the Lambtons, who, contrary to many warnings from local priests, insisted on fishing in the River Wear one Sunday. He only caught a small worm which, in contempt, he flung into a nearby well.

Soon afterwards he left for a Crusade to the Holy Land, but when he returned many months later he discovered, to his horror, that the creature had grown to a mighty dragon ('Worm' is the Old English word for a dragon), so large it could coil itself nine times around a local Wearside hill (still known as Worm Hill) and which needed the milk of nine cows each day to satisfy its hunger. Lambton sought the advice of a witch who told him how to kill the beast, providing he also killed the first living thing he saw afterwards. He slew the creature but, meeting his own father on his way back home, refused to commit patricide. In so doing, he condemned no less than nine generations of Lambtons to untimely deaths.

The power of the curse must have finally been exhausted, for in the 19th century John George Lambton, First Earl of Durham, received wide acclaim as one of the moving spirits behind the 1832 Reform Act, and his 1839 'Durham Report' on Canada is still seen as the germinating idea of the modern Commonwealth of Nations. A monument to 'Radical Jack', in the form of a Greek Temple, was built in 1844 on Penshaw Hill, alongside the present A183, and it remains a major Wearside landmark. It is now owned by the National Trust and can be viewed; there is a car park near by.

The origins of the macabre tale of the Lambton Worm are obscure, but it is not too fanciful to imagine the River Wear as a great serpent as it meanders its way into the old town and port of Sunderland. It was the river that provided the life-blood of the region, as the once bustling complexes of industry along both banks of the river testify, most of it linked to shipbuilding. Scores of specialist companies also served that industry by making marine engines, anchors, chains and ropes. You can enjoy much of this heritage along the new River Wear Trail, a 15-mile riverside walk from Fatfield, by the A182, through to Roker Pier in Sunderland. Alternatively, you can catch the River Wear Ferry operated by the passenger steamer, 'City of Norwich', which runs from Panns Bank, by Wearmouth Bridge, along the length of the Wear.

Though **Sunderland** still has two major working shipyards, most auxiliary equipment is now made throughout Britain and Europe, rather than being concentrated on local factories; but traces of this industrial past can still be seen. For example, Webster's Ropery, on the banks of the river near Deptford, was built by John Grimshaw and Rowland Webster in 1797 to exploit the latest rope-spinning technology of its day, invented by a local man, Richard Fothergill. The building is now a high technology training centre and workshop, with a pub and restaurant attached.

North Dock, or Wearmouth Dock, in Sunderland was designed by no less a figure than Isambard Kingdom Brunel, but was known as 'Sir Hedworth's bath tub' after its owner Sir Hedworth Williamson and because of its small size.

The Wear (or Wearmouth) Bridge, in the centre of town, was first erected in 1796 and was at that time the largest iron bridge in the world. It was replaced in 1859 by one designed by Robert Stephenson, which was in turn replaced by the present bridge, designed by Mott, Hay and Anderson in 1929.

Much of Sunderland's history is told in an exhibition in the Museum and Art Gallery in Borough Road, where you'll also find examples of the fine theatrical maritime paintings of Sunderland sailor and subsequent Royal Academy artist, Clarkson Stansfield.

The Grindon Museum in Sunderland occupies part of an Edwardian shipbuilder's house and re-creates the lifestyle of Edwardian Sunderland, when shipbuilding was at its height.

You'll find heritage of a different period at **Monkwearmouth**, also in Sunderland, where, at St Peter's Church, is one of the most important sites of early Christianity - a tiny Saxon church founded in 674AD by Benedict Biscop, a Northumbrian nobleman and thane of King Oswy, who had travelled to Rome and was inspired to found a monastery here. This was to become a great centre of culture and learning, rivalled only by nearby Jarrow, on the Tyne. The Venerable Bede, England's first great historian, lived and worked here for a time and described the monastery's foundation in his 'History of England'. The west tower and the wall of this most fascinating church have survived from Saxon times and the area around the church, close to shipyards, has been carefully landscaped.

Monkwearmouth also boasts one of the most handsome small railway stations in the British Isles, built in imposing neo-classical style to look more like a temple or a town hall. Trains no longer call there and it has now been converted into a small museum of the Victorian railway age.

Even more interesting for the railway historian is the Bowes Railway at **Springwell** village, north-east of **Washington.** It is the world's only standard-gauge, rope-hauled railway still in use and dates back to a George Stephenson colliery line of 1826, now restored as a tourist steam railway.

Washington, some six miles west of Sunderland, can claim to be the ancestral home of George Washington. Washington Old Hall was a manor house originally, built in the 12th century, and at least five generations of George Washington's direct ancestors lived there until 1288 and other members of the Washington family until 1613. The present house was rebuilt on the medieval foundations and, due for demolition in 1936, was saved and given to the National Trust, being officially re-opened by the American Ambassador in 1955. The ground floor and a bedroom have been furnished as a typical Durham manor house of the 17th and early-18th centuries. There is also a Jacobean rose garden.

Washington is also the home of the Washington Wildfowl and Wetlands Centre, a conservation area and birdwatchers' paradise covering some 100 acres of hillside and valley. There are over 1,200 birds representing no less than 105 different species, including Mallard, Wigeon, Pochard, Tufted Duck, Redshank, Lapwing and Heron. There is also the Peter Scott Visitor Centre, whose large picture windows overlook a succession of ponds in the Wear valley, and there are tea room and picnic areas and facilities for the disabled.

You can reach the centre by car (along the A195 and A1232), east of Washington, by bus or by river, the River Wear Ferry from Sunderland having a special stop at the centre. You can also walk there by riverside path through the James Steel Park, an area of woodland, farmland and open space alongside the River Wear, named after the man who was Lord Lieutenant of Tyne and Wear between 1974 and 1984.

It is worth making your way to **Roker**, immediately north of Sunderland, if only to visit St Andrew's Church in Talbot Road, described as 'the Cathedral of the Arts and Crafts Movement'. Built in 1906-1907, it was designed by Sir John Priestman, a local shipbuilder, and is crammed with treasures by the leading craftsmen of the period - silver lectern, pulpit and altar furniture by Ernest Gimson, the font by Randall Wells, stained-glass windows by H.A. Payne, chancel murals by Macdonald Gill, stone tablets engraved by Eric Gill, a Burne-Jones tapestry and carpets from the William Morris workshops.

Roker is a pleasant suburb, immediately to the north of the great breakwaters that form Sunderland's harbour. The northern breakwater, known as Roker Pier, is 2,709ft long and was opened in 1903. Roker Park has been carefully restored to its former Victorian splendour, and from Sunderland through Roker and Seaburn there is a six-mile-long seaside promenade which enjoys spectacular illuminations between August and November each year.

The coast between Roker and South Shields is scenically magnificent, with rocky cliffs projecting into the sea at Souter Point and Lizard Point and two impressive bays, Whitburn Bay and Marsden Bay. Marsden Rock is a huge natural 'arc de triomphe' in the sea, celebrated for its birdlife which include kittiwakes, fulmars and cormorants. A cliff lift links Marsden Grotto - a beach inn - with the top of the cliffs. This is an area rich in tales of smugglers and freebooters and colourful characters with names such as Willie the Rover, Peter the Hermit and Jack the Blaster.

Though so close to both Wearside and Tyneside, this coastline remains remarkably unspoiled and can be walked for all or part of the way, as there are frequent buses to take you back to a parked car.

No less a personage than King George V declared that the beach at South Shields was the finest he had seen. This is a stretch of fine firm sand behind which a small but pleasant resort thrives.

However, it is the older part of South Shields, now known with neighbouring areas as South Tyneside, that has given the town a new claim to fame, thanks to the work of one of the world's most popular novelists - Catherine Cookson.

Now in her eighties, Catherine Cookson has written a series of novels which captures the world of her own childhood, and that of her parents and grandparents, with vivid clarity. It is a world which was shaped in the early Industrial Revolution in the narrow streets and coal-mines, a world of class warfare and conflict, passion and tragedy, violence and reconciliation.

The mean streets she describes no longer exist. The old Town Hall is now part of a pedestrianised area, served by modern Metro railcars, and the town has a clean, modern image. A display in the town's museum in Ocean Road re-creates a South Shields home as it was when she was a child. You can buy her books there and souvenirs of her characters, some of whose names you'll see reflected in the shops and restaurants around the town - Catherine Cookson Country.

Arbeia Roman fort

In Baring Street you can see the extensive remains of the 2nd century Arbeia Roman fort, including gateway, fort wall and defences. The West Gate has been faithfully reconstructed to match what experts believe to be its original appearance, with two three-storey towers, two gates and side walls; the biggest reconstruction of its kind in the country, and a truly magnificent achievement.

Much of the old harbour area at South Shields is now being restored, particularly around the Mill Dam area along the riverside, where fine Georgian buildings and warehouses survive, and there is talk of a riverbus service to supplement the existing ferry service across the Tyne. The river itself, like all great river estuaries, is a constant fascination as boats, including the big Swedish passenger ferries, come around the breakwaters into the spectacular mouth of the Tyne heading for one of the great docks, a reminder of the importance of Newcastle as a port.

Mixed memories surround the town of **Jarrow,** further down the Tyne. Once the thriving centre for the Tyneside shipbuilding industry, it gained notoriety during the famous Jarrow Hunger March when hundreds of unemployed men from the area walked to London to draw attention to their plight. It was on The Slake, in Jarrow, as recently as the 1840s, that the last public gibbeting took place, leaving the body of an executed man to rot in irons - an event chronicled in Catherine Cookson's book, 'Katie Mulholland'.

Bede Monastery Museum, Jarrow Hall

Jarrow has a happier side, too, and that lies in its associations, like Monkwearmouth, with early Christianity. For it was here that Benedict

Biscop dedicated a second monastery, this time to St Paul, in 685AD. The original dedication stone can still be seen, together with a fragment of Anglo-Saxon stained glass which scientific tests have established to be the oldest ecclesiastical stained glass in Europe, if not the world. It was here that Bede wrote his great 'History of England'. Here also an ancient chair in the Chancel is reputed to have been used by Bede himself. At Bede Hall, a Georgian building near by, there are exhibitions and displays about the history of this remarkable community of scholars, and there are facsimiles of the early Bibles that were illuminated in manuscript here.

It's worth taking the ferry across the Tyne from South Shields to North Shields, perhaps linking by connecting bus and Metro to Tynemouth and Whitley Bay. Tyne and Wear, thanks to the brisk little yellow railcars of its Metro system, has one of the best public transport systems in the United Kingdom, which makes travelling much more fun than by car.

Tynemouth and **Whitley Bay** form a linked resort which is now all part of North Tyneside Metropolitan Borough. Overlooking the river at Tynemouth is the notable Collingwood Monument, the grand statue of Admiral Lord Collingwood (1748-1819), Nelson's second in command at Trafalgar, who went on to win the battle after Nelson's death. The four guns below the statue are from the 'Royal Sovereign', sister ship to the 'Victory'. Tynemouth Priory was built over the remains of a 7th century monastery which was the burial place of the Northumbrian kings. The castle was added in the 14th century to defend the priory, and later became important as a river and harbour fortification.

The Long Sands at Tynemouth lead on past **Cullercoats**, an old fishing village, to **Whitley Bay,** a seaside resort with a distinctly Edwardian charm, whose beaches and promenades lead to the lighthouse (now a museum) and St Mary's Island, now an important bird sanctuary.

The Holiday Inn is a modern complex situated just off the A1, slightly north of Newcastle, at **Seaton Burn** which, as well as being within easy reach of Northumbria's beautiful countryside and dramatic coastline, is packed with its own leisure facilities. The 150 excellently equipped and spacious bedrooms are complemented by a large indoor swimming pool, gymnasium, warm water whirlpool, saunas, solarium, games room and pool table. The Convivium Restaurant offers speciality and table d'hote carvery menus as well as a lounge menu, and the Mercury Bar, overlooking the swimming pool, is the perfect spot for a quiet drink with friends.

As well as being a superb base for holidaymakers, the Holiday Inn also has first class business facilities with conference rooms ranging from the Cheviot Suite, accommodating up to 400 delegates in a theatre-style layout, to the Commonwealth Room, providing for up to 60 delegates. Smaller rooms for meetings of up to 12 persons are also available.

Private functions such as wedding receptions and dinner dances also come within the scope of this AA listed and RAC recommended hotel; whatever your needs, the friendly and efficient staff will do their best to meet them at the Holiday Inn.

Holiday Inn

Two especially interesting places in North Tyneside are the Stephenson Railway Museum and the Wallsend Heritage Centre. The Stephenson Museum is at Middle Engine Lane, close to the colliery at Killingworth where George began his career as a humble engine-wright, and where his pioneering engine, 'Puffing Billy' - one of the earliest steam locomotives in the world - and many other relics are kept. The Wallsend Heritage Centre stands close to the Roman fort of Segedunum on Hadrian's Wall at Wallsend, with many Roman remains and material from excavations near by.

No visitor to Tyneside can avoid spending at least some time at the region's capital, Newcastle, one of Britain's most exciting cities. Positioned next to a great gorge in the River Tyne across which it is linked to its twin, Gateshead, by a series of impressive road and rail bridges, it contains many magnificent public buildings and an atmosphere which is difficult to describe.

Newcastle was and is many things - a Roman frontier station, a medieval fortress town with a 'new' castle built in 1080 as a base for the English army in the forages against the Scots in the 17th and 18th centuries, a great port, mining, engineering and shipbuilding centre and a focal point of the Industrial Revolution that changed the face of the world.

With so much to discover, where do you start? There's the castle itself and the city's medieval walls with a surviving gatehouse, The Black Gate, at Castle Garth; the cathedral, mainly 14th and 15th century; Blackfriars, former monastery and meeting place for medieval guilds, now a craft centre. There's the Quayside, now returning to life with imaginative restoration and new development. There's the superb central area of broad streets and shops and offices around Eldon Square and Gray's Monument, the central streets now pedestrianised but served by the underground Metro, so you can enjoy the scale of it all without the nuisance of traffic.

There's the modern civic centre which has won architectural awards. There's Leazes Park and the wonderful expanse of ancient common, the Town Moor. There's a whole cluster of museums and art galleries to fill any rainy day - the Laing Art Gallery, the Hatton Gallery, the Hancock Museum, the Museum of Antiquities, the Trinity Maritime Centre, the Museum of Science and Engineering, the Greek Museum, the Newburn Hall Motor Museum. There are the handsome suburbs around Jesmond and Gosforth, the broad shopping streets and elegant arcades, markets, pubs, cafes and restaurants.

None of these things can do justice to Newcastle's special sense of being a northern capital and, above all else, having a feeling of energy and vitality that comes from the people - the true Geordies - whose sharp wit and perception make Newcastle one of the great cities of England and indeed Europe.

Conveniently situated off the A696 and just a short distance from Newcastle Airport, the **Wheatsheaf Hotel** enjoys a delightful rural setting. Soldiers once billeted here will no longer recognise this elegant and stylish place, which has been awarded the coveted five crowns by the Tourist Board. The accommodation is luxurious, with all modern conveniences, and rooms have been thoughtfully designed with facilities for families and disabled visitors. Children are well catered for and there is an excellent play area to keep them occupied.

Alan and Mandy McIntosh Reid offer the very best in cuisine and atmosphere to suit all tastes and moods. In the formal Callerton Restaurant, where chandeliers and crystal tinkle, table d'hote and a la carte include smoked salmon, game, magre duck, monkfish and asparagus. Here, lucky newly-weds can enjoy a reception to be remembered - and there is a lovely garden for photographs! The Rendezvous is more informal and on two levels, the lower leading down to the garden. The menu offers a selection of dishes in three courses as well as the popular Brewers Fayre. A convenient sandwich is always available at the Woolsington Bar. There are certainly a few surprises to be experienced at the Wheatsheaf: everyone will enjoy the excellent hospitality and quality at very reasonable prices, but an appearance by the 'Callerton Poacher' is sure to leave some guests startled in quite another way.

The Wheatsheaf Hotel

Gateshead has perhaps suffered from proximity to its big sister, Newcastle, for generations but, thanks to the new Metro Centre, one of the largest and most impressive shopping and leisure complexes in Western Europe, the borough is very much on the map as a place where Tynesiders and many other people go - not just to shop, but for entertainment in various forms. Gateshead was also the site of the 1990 Garden Festival, and the town boasts some fine parks and gardens.

There are some surprisingly lovely areas of countryside to explore within Gateshead Borough; a mixture of natural beauty and cultural history, including industrial heritage.

Through the creative use of, for example, derelict land and disused railway track, the Gateshead area now offers much more than light industry and intensive shopping - the simple joys of the countryside are available too, and perhaps the best place to start would be down on the farm.

Bill Quay Community Farm, for example, is set on the banks of the river Tyne to the east of Gateshead. The farm is a Rare Breed Centre and has a national reputation for its work in conserving rare breeds of livestock such as Old Spot, Saddleback and Tamworth pigs, multi-horned Jacobs sheep and English Longhorn cattle. The purpose-built farm unit, opened in 1985, is a model on which many other similar projects throughout the country have been based, and it is a valuable teaching resource for local schools. Visitors are encouraged to feed and look after the animals, and the friendly staff are happy to answer questions.

Bill Quay Community Farm

The farm site includes a wild flower meadow, a butterfly house, a craft and information centre (which hosts day-long workshops of various kinds) and a Sculpture Park where visitors can try their hand at creating their own sculptures.

Bill Quay Farm is open to the public daily and admission is free; the Saddleback Coffee Rooms are open at weekends.

Saltwell Park, more centrally situated, is, at 55 acres, one of the largest parks in the north-east of England and combines stunning displays and quiet walks through mature woodland. Horticulturalists will admire the Victorian bedding plants, traditional rose garden, heather garden and maze; the variety of planting ensures a continual blaze of colour. The lake is host to a wealth of waterfowl and the park has a formal aviary. There are rowing boats for hire as well as a paddle steamer.

Saltwell Park

More energetic activities include tennis, crazy golf and bowls, with mini-motorbikes and an inflatable castle for the children. A particularly impressive attraction is the Vickers Viscount aircraft which can be 'flown'. Fairs and circuses regularly visit Saltwell Park and, whatever the time of year, visitors can be assured of a pleasant day out.

Central Nursery at Lobley Hill

The Central Nursery at **Lobley Hill** is one of the most modern in the country. Opened in 1985 by H.R.H. the Duke of Kent, it is a centre of horticultural excellence which provides all the plants, trees and shrubs for the Metropolitan Borough of Gateshead, and which has achieved some notable successes in the 'Britain in Bloom' competitions. The eight glasshouses, covering 3,034 square metres, have computer-controlled heating systems.

An important part of the service offered at the Central Nursery is plant information for the general public, and this service is based in the showhouse which has pools, fish and ornamental planting. Visitors can also enjoy the herb garden, rose garden, heather and conifer garden and tree and shrub nursery. A special picnic area has tables and chairs.

The Derwent Walk Country Park covers 350 acres of woodland and riverside meadow, and the Derwent Walk is the track bed of the old Derwent Valley Railway between Swalwell and Consett. The three and a half miles (and surrounding country park) which are in the care of the Metropolitan Borough Council of Gateshead run from Swalwell, over the Nine Arches Viaduct, to Rowlands Gill, and this imaginatively converted bridleway forms a focus for Gateshead's area of unspoiled countryside. The main walk (which is suitable for cycles, horses and wheelchairs) gives access to a number of paths which include nature trails (two of which start at Thornley Woodlands Centre in the heart of Thornley Wood), the South Tyne Cycleway and the Heritage Way. Swalwell Visitor Centre, situated at the northern end of the Derwent Walk, is the starting point for a history trail. This centre also has a large pond and butterfly garden.

Derwent Walk Country Park

Situated in a secluded valley at Rowlands Gill (which has another Information Centre) is the Derwent Park Caravan and Camping Site, open from April to September. The site has excellent facilities which include a shower block, laundry, shop and electric hook-up points. Advanced booking is advisable at this site for Bank Holidays. Leisure opportunities provided here include tennis, bowls, mini-golf, riverside picnic area, children's playground and day permit trout fishing.

Just west of Swalwell at **Blaydon** on the B6317 is Shibdon Pond, one of the few open-water sites on Tyneside. A footpath gives access to the marsh and grassland beyond the pond, and a specially constructed ride gives excellent views of the many different water-birds. Already well known to specialist birdwatchers, Shibdon Pond is becoming increasingly popular with the general public.

Central Northumberland

Otterburn Tower
CHAPTER SEVEN

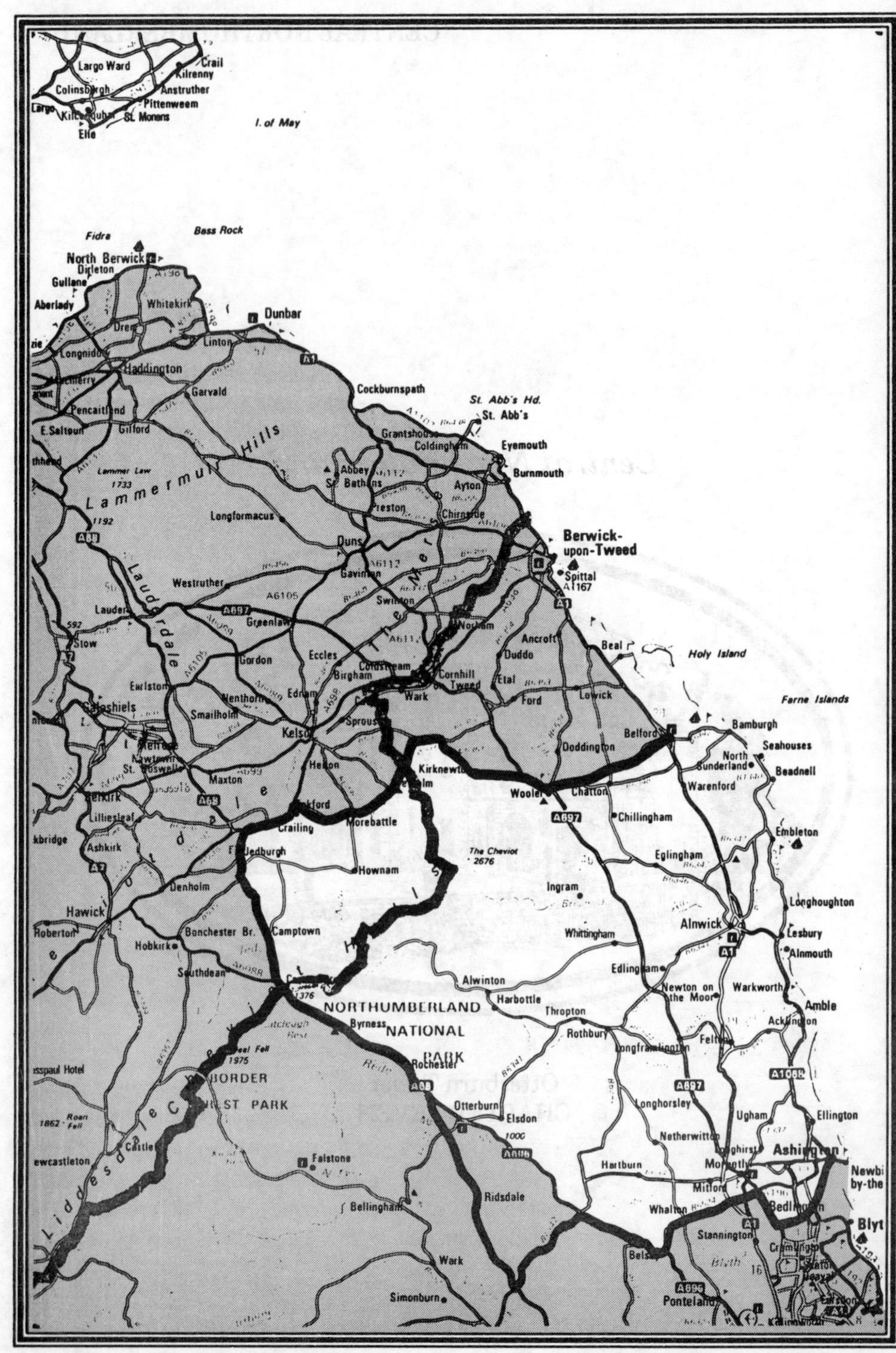

Largo Ward
Crail
Kilrenny
Colinsburgh
Anstruther
Pittenweem
St. Monans
Elie
I. of May
Fidra
Bass Rock
North Berwick
Dirleton
Gullane
Aberlady
Whitekirk
Dunbar
Linton
Haddington
Garvald
Cockburnspath
St. Abb's Hd.
St. Abb's
Pencaitland
E. Saltoun
Gifford
Grantshouse
Coldingham
Eyemouth
Lammer Law
1733
Lammermuir Hills
Abbey St. Bathans
Burnmouth
Ayton
Longformacus
Preston
Chirnside
1192
Berwick-upon-Tweed
Duns
Spittal
Westruther
Gavinton
A6105
Swinton
Lauderdale
Lauder
Greenlaw
A697
Norham
Ancroft
Stow
Beal
Holy Island
Gordon
Eccles
Duddo
Coldstream
Birgham
Cornhill on Tweed
Earlston
Edram
Etal
Wark
Lowick
Ford
Farne Islands
Galashiels
Smailholm
Kelso
Bamburgh
Seahouses
Belford
North Sunderland
Beadnell
Doddington
Kirknewton
Wooler
Chatton
Warenford
Maxton
Chillingham
Embleton
Crailing
Morebattle
Ashkirk
Jedburgh
The Cheviot
2676
Eglingham
Hownam
Ingram
Longhoughton
Denholm
Hawick
Alnwick
Robertor
Lesbury
Bonchester Br.
Camptown
Whittingham
Hobkirk
Alnmouth
Southdean
Edlingham
Alwinton
Newton on the Moor
Warkworth
Harbottle
NORTHUMBERLAND NATIONAL PARK
Thropton
Amble
Byrness
Rothbury
Felton
Rochester
BORDER FOREST PARK
Otterburn
Longhorsley
Elsdon
Ugham
Ellington
Roan Fell
Castleton
Netherwitton
Falstone
Ashington
Hartburn
Mitford
Ridsdale
Bellingham
Whalton
Bedlington
Stannington
Wark
Belsay
Simonburn
Ponteland
Liddesdale
A1
A68
A7
A697
A1068
A696

Chapter Seven - Map Reference Guide
Central Northumberland

Kielder Water Restaurant - Kielder Water

Kielder Bikes - Kielder Water

Roseden Farm Shop - Wooperton

Breamish Country House Hotel - Powburn

The Tone Inn - Birtley

Newcastle Hotel - Rothbury

Bird in Bush Inn - Elsdon

Otterburn Mill - Otterburn

Ravenshill - Kielder

Old Post Office Cottage - Little Bavington

Thorneyburn Lodge - Greenhaugh

The Bay Horse Inn - West Woodburn

The Anglers Arms - Weldon Bridge

The Salmon Inn - Holystone

Ogle House Guest House & Restaurant - Eglingham

Belsay

CHAPTER SEVEN

Central Northumberland

The 398 square miles of the Northumberland National Park occupy much of central Northumberland, stretching from Tynedale to the Scottish Border. This is the least populated, and perhaps the least well known, of Britain's 11 National Parks, an area of remote, wild, and hauntingly beautiful, upland countryside.

The most famous feature of these uplands are The Cheviot Hills, a range of magnificent, round-topped, grass-covered hills, which rise to the summit of The Cheviot itself, at 2,674ft. Quiet valleys radiate from the central hills through which streams sparkle and scattered woods of oak, birch and rowan contrast with the bare summits of the hills.

To the south of the main Cheviot massif lie two other impressive hill-ranges, the Simonside and Harbottle hills, both consisting largely of sandstone, which rise to gentle, flat-topped summits on which there are large areas of heather moorland and forest. This is an area linked to the activities of prehistoric man and, for anyone with time, patience, a good pair of boots and a large-scale map, there are stone circles, standing stones and cup-and-ring marked rocks to be discovered, together with the remains of Iron Age and Roman settlements.

To the east lies a region of great forests - Redesdale Forest, Kielder Forest and the other associated areas that form the massive Border Forest Park, the largest area of man-made forest in Britain. If that were not enough, there is also the vast expanse of Wark Forest to the south. Kielder Water, to add to this list of superlatives, is the largest man-made lake in northern Europe, covering 2,684 acres with 27 miles of shoreline and containing 44,000 billion gallons of water which serve the domestic and industrial needs of Tyneside.

Kielder Water has become one of the most popular areas for informal countryside recreation in Northumberland. It is probably best to start from the excellent Visitor Centre at Tower Knowe, on the south side of the lake and reached by forest-road from Bellingham. Exhibitions tell the story of the creation of the lake and how it has changed the environment of the region. The attraction of Kielder Water lies in its ability to provide so much to see and do in an area surrounded by a refreshing sense of freedom.

Complementing the many recreational facilities available here, you will find **Kielder Water Restaurant**. This modern restaurant, sitting on the banks of the water, lies adjacent to Tower Knowe Visitor Centre and offers an extensive range of refreshments - choose anything, from a light snack to a four course meal.

The restaurant is open between 10am and 6pm daily. Traditional and vegetarian dishes are served, with a full range of soft drinks available to suit all the family.

Proprietors Sylvia Bertie and Arthur Hughes stress that the disabled can and do use the restaurant with relative ease, and public toilets are available within a few hundred yards of the tearoom.

Among the many visitors to Kielder Water Restaurant, well-known patrons include Norman Wisdom, Jimmy Shand and Jack Charlton - so we're sure you'll agree that all types are well looked after here!

Whether relaxing after an exhilarating day out or breaking a journey, enjoy a satisfying meal and take in the commanding views across the water and forest.

Kielder Water Restaurant

The main water-sports and activities centre is at Leaplish, with lakeside and woodland walks, and a forest playground for children. Bathekin Reservoir, in the northern section, is reserved for nature conservation, whilst walkers can follow the viaduct which once carried the North Tyne Railway, and is now a superb viewpoint.

Kielder Bikes offers the pleasurable experience of exploring, at a leisurely pace, the many sights and sounds of the countryside around the reservoir. A helpful guide gives details of a series of cycle routes following quiet country lanes, old bridleways and forest tracks, away from the traffic.

The routes are planned so that cyclists can enjoy varied scenery, delightful villages and sleepy hamlets with excellent hostelries, historic sites and a wealth of wildlife. Party bookings can be made in off-peak periods and there is a range of bikes to suit all ages.

Kielder Bikes

Kielder itself is a Forestry Commission village that was built in the 1950s to house workers in Kielder Forest.

Less than a mile from Kielder, a warm welcome awaits the visitors on holiday at **Ravenshill.** At the end of a half-mile, tree-lined drive from Kielder castle stands an imposing country house built in the mid-19th century as the residence of the Duke of Northumberland's Land Agent. Commanding an elevated position, the rooms enjoy splendid panoramic views of the forested slopes of the upper North Tyne valley.

Ann and Peter Coffey operate a small, family run guest house and restaurant where visitors may enjoy excellent home cooking either as a snack or a satisfying meal, or even indulge in a fresh cream tea, at perhaps a higher cost to waistline than pocket. As a speciality option guests may take advantage of Ann and Peter's guided rides through the forest, or even, by prior arrangement, bring their own horse on holiday with them, such is the range of accommodation.

Other activities include good fishing and a range of water sports on Kielder Water. There are many historic places to visit and Ravenshill is an ideal centre for touring and exploring the Borders.

Ravenshill

The sheer scale of Kielder contrasts with the more intimate landscape of the small towns and villages on the edge of the National Park, and in the three major valleys which cut into the hills. These were formed by the River Tyne and its major tributary, the Rede (forming Redesdale), and to the north, the beautiful valley of the Coquet which runs across to Amble on the coast.

Thorneyburn Lodge nestles among a collection of isolated farms in a magnificent setting overlooking the valley of the Tarset Burn. While numerous peles and castles will remind visitors of the area's turbulent history, when border raiding was the principal occupation, today the countryside is lulled by its tranquillity and 'the natives', promises Margaret Robertson, 'are more than friendly'.

Originally the village school, Thorneyburn Lodge has now been converted to offer excellent accommodation for a small number of guests. Facilities include en-suite, well-equipped bedrooms, a spacious lounge (which was once the schoolroom) with an open log fire, television, audio equipment and a piano, and a charming dining room. Margaret personally supervises all the freshly prepared dishes; dinner, which is available every night, consists of five courses.

A sun-porch leads to a large, well-maintained garden and visitors wishing to venture beyond can explore the Kielder Forest and Northumbrian fells or enjoy the many water-sports at Kielder Water. The adjacent hamlet, Greenhaugh, has no shops but does boast an authentic Northumbrian Pub.

Thorneyburn Lodge

The North Tyne is fed by Kielder Water, and on its way down to join the South Tyne above Hexham, passes two interesting villages, Bellingham and Wark. **Bellingham** is actually a small market town, in a moorland setting, with a broad main street and market place, and an austere little church, reflecting the constant troubles of the area in medieval times. The roof was twice burned by the Scots and required a massive stone roof, supported by stone ribs, to reduce risk of arson.

In the churchyard at Bellingham, an oddly-shaped tomb stone somewhat reminiscent of a pedlar's pack is associated with a foiled robbery attempt that took place in 1723. A pedlar arrived at Lee Hall, a former mansion between Bellingham and Wark, and asked if he could be put up for the night. As her master was away at the time the maid felt bound to refuse, but told the pedlar that he could leave his heavy pack at the Hall and collect it the next day. Imagine her consternation when some time later the pack began to move! Hearing her screams for help, a servant rushed to the scene and fired his gun at the moving bundle. When blood poured out of the pack and the body of an armed man was discovered inside, the servants realised that this had been a clever attempt to burgle the Hall. They sounded a horn which they found inside the pack next to the body, and when the robber's accomplices came running in response to the prearranged signal, they were speedily dealt with by the servants who lay in wait for them.

The Bay Horse Inn

Some four miles north-east of here is the **Bay Horse Inn** in **West Woodburn**; a very attractive, Grade II listed 18th century coaching inn. The obvious advantage of the Inn is that it is situated on the main A68 scenic tourist route. Visitors are therefore extremely well placed to explore as far afield as the Border Country, Hadrian's Wall, Kielder Water and the coast. Behind the Inn is the River Rede, where with a bit of luck and patience, anglers can catch trout and salmon. Owners John and Irenee Cowans provide very comfortable accommodation, and one of the five guest rooms even boasts a four poster bed. The restaurant can seat up to 32 diners, and the a la carte menu offers a wide choice of dishes. We are curious to know if any of the local fish end up on your plate! Breakfast, lunch and an evening meal are all provided and John is justifiably proud of the extensive wine list. In the three and a half years they have been here, John and Irenee have certainly made it into a great place to relax before tackling the long stretches that lay ahead.

There is a spacious children's play area equipped with swings and slides, a barbecue area, and in the well stocked garden, we were intrigued to find a Roman mile stone. Many visitors from abroad pass through here so you may hear American and Swedish voices - as well as those like us from not so far away, who come in search of Northumberland's mystery.

Wark, to the south of Bellingham, is an attractive estate village, once part of the lordship of Wark; the Scottish kings are said to have held court here in the 12th century. Birtley, across the river, is another attractive village that was entirely rebuilt by the Dukes of Northumberland in the last century.

The Tone Inn, near **Birtley,** has always been something of an oasis on this main route to Scotland. On the long trek to the Borders, the busy road runs for many miles in a straight line, revealing its Roman origins. It passes through attractive countryside, but the succession of hills, almost like a switchback, allows little opportunity for the traveller to rest. This inn is therefore as welcome a sight today as it must have been in the 17th century when it was primarily a coaching inn on the sole eastern route to Scotland and the borders. Unfortunately, the origin of the unusual name is now a mystery.

The Tone Inn

These days it provides a centre for the rural community, and locals and travellers thoroughly enjoy Sinclair and Sheila Russell's wide range of refreshments from snacks and pub meals to steaks. On Sunday lunchtimes visitors can feast themselves on a carvery of ample proportions!

On the slopes overlooking the North Tyne are a large number of prehistoric settlements, many of them with picturesque names such as Male Knock Camp, Good Wife Camp, Nigh Folds Camp, Carryhouse Camp and Shieldence Camp; names probably given to the monuments by itinerant gypsies in former times.

Coquetdale, to the north, forms perhaps the ideal starting point for a visit to central Northumberland. The Coquet has the reputation of being one of the finest salmon rivers in England, twisting its way down from high on the Cheviots, past the village of Alwinton at the head of the dale.

Alwinton, a cluster of stone and slate cottages and farms in a deep fold of the hills, has all the feeling of a little frontier outpost, situated as it is where an ancient drovers' road, Clennel Street, comes over from the Scottish border into England. The name of the village inn, the Rose and Thistle, recalls an allegiance to both England and Scotland, and Sir Walter Scott once stayed here. The church at Low Alwinton is built, unusually, on two levels, and dates from the 12th century.

The village's remote setting, away from the watchful eyes of the excise men and with plenty of peaty water from local burns, made it a popular place for illicit whisky stills. 'Rory's Still', marked by a few rocks beside the Usway Burn, remained in use until last century.

You can still see the grass-covered terraces on the hillside where oats were once grown, and this is an area rich in hill forts and prehistoric circles.

Harbottle is another delightful Coquetdale village of traditional cottages, lying in a sheltered hollow. Close to the village you can see the ruins of Harbottle Castle, originally founded in 1160 by King Henry II and the Bishop of Durham, as a border outpost to guard the pass. The Drake Stone, a great 30ft high, reddish-grey, sandstone boulder on the hillside about half a mile above the village, was, in former times, presumed to have magic powers and sick children were carried over it in an effort to help their recovery.

Holystone, also on the south of the Coquet, is tucked away in a beautifully secluded setting five miles west of Rothbury, and just off the B6341. It has two holy wells, St Mungo's and St Ninian's, the latter in a small grove of fir trees and known as the Lady's Well, now owned by the National Trust. It was here at Easter 627AD that St Paulinus was reputed to have baptised over 3,000 Northumbrians. There was a 12th century nunnery nearby; the Church of St Mary stands on the site and some fragments of stonework from the nunnery were used for the rebuilt church.

The Salmon Inn is the ideal place to break your journey through this quiet Northumbrian backwater. John and Sylvia Gilbertson will offer you an extremely warm welcome to their village inn - and don't worry if you've brought the children, for their welcome is also extended to families.

This lovely old inn dates back to the 16th century and has seen 400 years of Northumbrian history and life. Look around and you will see original oak beams and tapestry furniture. The open fireplace is listed and hides a priesthole, used as a hiding place for monks during the persecutions of the 16th century.

John and Sylvia offer an excellent range of home cooked bar meals, available at lunchtime and in the evenings. A feature sadly lacking in many village inns is the opportunity to take children inside for a meal. This, however, is where the Salmon Inn comes out on top, for they have a special children's menu which will suit everyone's budget - a nice touch, which makes things easier for everyone.

The Salmon Inn is certainly well worth seeking out, in its haven of peace and tranquillity. As the saying goes - try it, you'll be glad you did!

The Salmon Inn

Hepple, on the B6341, has another reminder of the difficulty of life near the borders in the form of Hepple Tower, a 14th century pele tower built so strongly that attempts to demolish it, to use the stone for a new farmhouse, had to be abandoned. This is also an area of exceptionally interesting prehistoric earthworks, including several hill forts.

Thropton has an attractive early-18th century inn, and Thropton Tower is a particularly good example of a Northumbrian, early-15th century Bastle-House or fortified farm, first mentioned in documents as far back as 1415.

Rothbury is a natural focal point from which to explore Coquetdale. A small town, former Victorian spa and attractive tourist centre, with attractive stone houses and tree-lined streets, it can trace its origins to before the Norman Conquest and enjoys a superb setting in the centre of the dale.

It is also an excellent starting-point for some delightful walks along valley or hillside or through forest, the most famous perhaps being to the summit of Simonside, a fine viewpoint, or along the Rothbury Terraces, a series of parallel tracks along the hillside above the town, which also offer superb views.

The Newcastle Hotel in Rothbury faces onto the peaceful gardens of the war memorial. It was built in 1687, just two years after the death of Charles II. Even here, memories of England under Oliver Cromwell, who had died almost 30 years before, will have raised a few doubts about the future under this new king.

Newcastle Hotel

Although it was originally a coaching inn, the external appearance is more that of a substantial civic building (as its name implies) than the conventional image of a coaching inn which is popularly conveyed on Christmas cards.

The pleasant restaurant has a cottage-style decor, and the specialities are 18oz T-bone steaks and the chef's own homemade Chicken Kiev.

Food is also available in the bar, and the menu here is rather more than the usual traditional bar snacks: roast half-duckling a l'orange is not normally available as a bar snack!

In addition to the present residential accommodation of five comfortable bedrooms, Jean and Jim Routledge are planning another seven rooms.

Only a short distance from Rothbury is Cragside, a magnificent National Trust property, once the home of Sir William Armstrong, the inventor and industrialist. Armstrong - a pioneer of the turbine - developed his own hydro-electric system with man-made lakes, streams and miles of underground piping. The huge Victorian house was largely designed by Norman Shaw in a style which was partly Elizabethan and partly Gothic. It was completed in 1880 and has been beautifully restored and furnished. Among many fine rooms is the library with some William Morris glass in the bay windows, and the drawing room with a 20ft-high mantlepiece of richly carved marble. The 900-acre country park is celebrated for its miles of walkways and superb displays of shrubs and rhododendrons.

There are now exhibition areas and a wide range of visitor facilities, including a restaurant, disabled facilities, and a children's playground.

To the east of Rothbury on the A697, Longframlington owes its name to its founder, one Walter de Framlington, who founded the church in 1190. Many original features of Walter's church remain, including a graceful chancel arch.

Nearby Brinkburn Priory, on the Coquet, was also established in the late-12th century and may have been built by the same masons who constructed Longframlington church. It is in a beautiful setting and was painted by Turner as a romantic ruin, but its church was restored as a private chapel in later years and has many fine architectural features, including some lofty lancet windows. A round Norman font may also be seen.

Weldon Bridge, only a short distance away, has an exceptionally elegant five-arched bridge across the River Coquet, dating from 1744 which, though it no longer carries the main road, remains an impressive feature.

The Anglers Arms at Weldon Bridge is a Grade II listed building which dates from the 1760s when it was an important coaching inn. At the time of our visit, five-bedroom accommodation was being offered, but the planned expansion to 32 bedrooms should now be complete. The Anglers Arms has an excellent reputation for food and serves table d'hote, a la carte and bar meals, together with a wide selection of beers, lagers and wines.

Linked to the main building - which has its own restaurant - is a Pullman railway carriage dining-car: an unusual and luxurious setting in which to enjoy fine local meat, fresh sea-food from Northumberland fishing villages and game shot by local sportsmen.

Set in a lovely valley surrounded by forest, the Anglers Arms provides both a comfortable base from which to explore the region and a warm and friendly atmosphere for guests who merely want to relax. Visitors to the hotel may like to take advantage of the fishing - free of charge to residents.

Whatever your requirements, Mike Rudd, the enterprising young director, together with his enthusiastic staff, will offer an amiable welcome and excellent service.

The Anglers Arms

The third of the major valleys in this part of Northumberland, Redesdale, is a wilder, remoter valley than the Coquet, the River Rede branching from the North Tyne, east of Bellingham, coming down from its source in Redesdale Forest.

Byrness, a small village at the top end of Redesdale, not far from Catcleugh Reservoir and Carter Bar on the Scottish Border, is a good base from which to explore the border country. Ramshope Burn, which flows into the reservoir, is celebrated for its polished pebbles of yellow, red and bluish-white jasper, whilst Bateinghope Burn is celebrated as the tragic setting for 'The Ballad of Percy Reed'. The Pennine Way goes through the village on its final stage to Kirk Yetholm.

Rochester, as its name implies, was a Roman camp on Dere Street, and this is an area rich in archaeological remains, including the camp at High Rochester or Bremenium. This is considered to be one of the finest Roman forts of its kind in Britain, an outstation several miles north of Hadrian's Wall.

Otterburn commands a strategic position in Upper Redesdale, where the main A696 trunk road crosses the wild expanse of Rayless Common into Redesdale on its route through the borders to Jedburgh and Scotland. It was once an important coaching town where horses were changed.

There was a time when almost all the villages around here had their local Mills, harnessing the water power of the little streams to grind corn or to waulk cloth. At least five in the surrounding valley were corn mills, but at Otterburn the clear soft water was utilised for washing and dyeing the wools as well as for fulling and consolidating the handwoven, homespun cloths.

The history of **Otterburn Mill** goes back at least 600 years, the earliest mention of it being in 1245. Situated in the valley bottom it must have witnessed many border skirmishes; for instance, the Battle of Otterburn which was fought less than a mile away in August 1388 between the locally raised armies of the Douglas on the Scots side and the Percys of Northumberland. The 5,000 strong Scottish army was pursued by an English army under the leadership of Henry Percy, better known as 'Hotspur' of Shakespearean fame. Although the English were defeated and Percy was captured, it was not before the Scottish leader, James, Earl of Douglas, had been killed by Percy in a dual. The place where Douglas died was said to be marked by an upright, pointed pillar known as Percy's Cross. It now stands in a clump of fir trees by the main road, just north of Otterburn, having been moved there after a road diversion in 1777. The events are recalled in the ancient 'Border Ballad of Otterbourne'.

Mr Justice Hall - better known as 'Mad Jack' - was Lord of the Manor owning Otterburn Mill in 1707, but he later lost his head at Tyburn and forfeited his estates for his suspected support of the Jacobite cause. As was the case with much of the land around this vulnerable border area, constant protection from the Scots invaders was an everyday necessity. In 1522, in fact, it is recorded that the fords here were to be guarded nightly against any potential marauders.

The present family's connection with Otterburn Woollen Mill starts with the elopement of 17-year-old Charlotte Ferrier from her school in Edinburgh with one William Waddell from Jedburgh. The young family took over the Mill in 1821 and over the generations added spinning, weaving and finishing processes to the traditional fulling and dyeing. The last 100 years have seen many changes in the scale and type of operation of this family business. Today Otterburn is synonymous with quality and design in tasteful tweeds - and generations of mothers wouldn't be without their Otterburn pram rug!

An extensive display of tweeds greets the visitor to the Mill Showroom. There are cosy rugs in a profusion of colourways and sizes. The skirt department teams tweed garments with fine lambswool co-ordinating sweaters. Chunky Aran, Motif styles and Icelandic soft brushed sweaters are all available. There are wraps and scarves, tweed hats, knitted bonnets, sheepskin rugs, slippers, gloves, and numerous gift items.

We certainly recommend that you come and explore this famous showroom and its village surrounded by rolling fells on the edge of Northumberland National Park. Otterburn is easy to reach and the beauty of the countryside around here is a reward in itself.

Otterburn Mill

It is worth making the short journey from Otterburn to Elsdon, the historic capital of Redesdale, where many of the dead from the Battle of Otterburn were taken for burial. It became the headquarters of the Marches Lords of Redesdale in the 12th century, and it also lay on the old drove-road between Scotland and Newcastle. The great Mote Hills, just behind the village, are remains of a Norman motte and bailey castle. Elsdon Tower is a pele tower dating from 1400 and the church of St Cuthbert goes back to the 14th century and has some unusual vaulting in the aisles.

A visit to the **Bird in Bush Inn** at **Elsdon** may turn out to be an experience not easily forgotten! In this charming 17th century, grade II listed building, Walter and Linda Parker run a popular pub and restaurant and offer limited accommodation.

In the cosy and traditionally-decorated interior, fascinating details include carved wood panelling in the bar originating from a Dutch cargo ship two centuries ago, and a large collection of foreign currency which adorns the exposed beams. During past renovations a child's boot fell out of the chimney, and it is said that the mischievious owner occasionally returns to retrieve this item - in spirit! The inn's ghost is just one of the bizarre stories of Elsdon.

Bird in Bush Inn

East of the A68 - Roman Dere Street - and north of the Tyne lies an area of gentle, undulating countryside of scattered woodland and rich farmland

which includes several exceptionally lovely villages. Among these are Stamfordham; Hartburn, which is situated where the Roman road to the Tweed crossed a deep, wooded ravine; Bywell with its two churches; Matfen with its gracious park and delightful cottage gardens; Kirkwhelpington where the great marine engineer Sir Charles Parsons lies buried and Belsay with its superb neo-Grecian Hall, built in 1810-17 to the designs of Sir Charles Monk. Belsay Hall is now owned and managed by English Heritage. A quiet network of lanes links these villages, making it an ideal area to explore at leisure, away from the busy tourist trails. There is a small country park with picnic places and theme trails around Bolam Lake, near Belsay.

The tiny hamlet of **Little Bavington** lies mid-way between the A68 and A696 on the B6342, near Hallington Reservoir. It is set right in the heart of Bobby Shafto country and is close to many 'musts' for interested sightseers. These include Wallington Hall, Cragside, Belsay Hall and Castle, Warkworth Castle, Hadrian's Wall and many more.

Old Post Office Cottage

At **Old Post Office Cottage,** Christine Rodger - a Scottish exile - and her family love to share their home with their guests. Christine prides herself on the homemade evening meals she offers. Northumbrian venison and rainbow trout as big as the one that got away (caught by husband John) feature regularly on the menu. As a lover of vegetarian food herself, she also offers an interesting range of such dishes. We found the food to be home cooking at its very best.

The choice of bedrooms includes a large pleasant family room (with a cot available if required) and a pretty twin-bedded room. The charming lounge has a welcoming log fire, the dining room is spacious, and both rooms have beamed ceilings.

We thought that this would make an excellent base from which to explore the beautiful countryside and spectacular beaches of this part of Northern England.

Somewhere not to be missed in any visit to this part of Northumberland is **Cambo**, an 18th century estate village close to Wallington House and Park, two miles to the east of Kirkwhelpington. This elegant house, now owned by the National Trust, occupies the site of a medieval castle and was built in 1688 and altered in the 1740s. It has outstanding plasterwork and collections of fine porcelain, elegant furnishings and paintings, a collection of dolls' houses, and a display of coaches. Outside, there are a walled terrace garden, a conservatory and spacious parkland.

The main A697 between Morpeth and Wooler skirts the edge of the Cheviots, past remote villages including Powburn - whose name comes from the Scottish, meaning 'slow stream' - where the ancient Roman road (known as the 'Devil's Causeway') between Newcastle and the Tweed, crosses through the village.

Breamish Country House Hotel

Situated at **Powburn,** the **Breamish Country House Hotel** is an elegant Georgian-style building which started life as a farmhouse in 1650 and was converted to a much grander hunting lodge in the 1800s. Its 10 guest rooms - which bear charming names such as Sycamore, Cherry and Willow - are impeccably appointed and offer the visitor total comfort and privacy. The hotel is set in five acres of garden and woodland in the heart of the Northumbrian countryside but within easy reach of the unspoilt coast.

Breamish Country House Hotel has a well-earned reputation for superb meals prepared by cooks trained to Cordon Bleu standard and has been recognized in many major food guides; dipping into a typical dinner menu provides several treats: salmon and prawns in a piquant mayonnaise sauce served in a basket of filo pastry; cream of parsnip soup; roast loin of lamb cooked with garlic, lusciously stuffed with herbs, orange and nuts and served with apple mint jelly.

Understandably, this hotel is AA and RAC recommended.

You can find your way along quiet cul-de-sac lanes that wind deep into secret valleys from where the only way forward is on foot, along hill-tracks and paths.

By taking the lane north of Powburn, for example, along the valley of the little River Breamish, you soon reach the charming village of **Ingram**, with a church dating back to Edward the Confessor. The modern village lies close to a prehistoric settlement, whilst the road through the village ends in a deep mountain gorge. There is a National Park Information Centre in Ingram, a popular starting-point for walks onto the high fells.

Eglingham village sits on the B6436, six miles north of Alnwick and on the road to Wooler. This picturesque village boasts a beautiful Norman church and is the perfect base for walking, touring and just enjoying the peace and tranquillity of this area.

Visitors to Eglingham seeking quality accommodation in comfortable surroundings need look no further than **Ogle House Guest House and Restaurant**. Built around 1790 as a coaching inn, this stone-built Grade II listed building has been tastefully renovated to provide a high standard of comfort. For their efforts, proprietors Norman and Carol Ann McRoberts hold a three coronet award from the English Tourist Board.

There are three guest rooms available, all comfortably furnished and with full en-suite facilities. Parents with young children will be pleased to know that baby listening devices are also provided.

Norman and Carol Ann strive to provide their guests with only the best in fresh local produce, served in their cosy restaurant, which is also open to non-residents. A typical menu may include homemade soup, fresh locally caught salmon with vegetables, and fresh cream gateau with coffee to follow. A table license is pending, for those of you who enjoy a drink with your meal.

If you're looking for a special gift to take home, or simply wish to treat yourself, you'll find a marvellous selection of original gifts available in the McRoberts' adjoining Ogle House Craft Shop.

All in all, you will find that this charming couple will do all they can to make your stay in Eglingham as pleasant as possible.

Ogle House Guest House & Restaurant

Another village well worth discovering is **Whittingham**, through the centre of which runs the little River Aln. This is yet another ancient settlement, probably dating back to the Bronze Age. The church has Anglo-Saxon remains; there is a 14th century pele tower and a former coaching inn.

Three miles to the north of Powburn and just off the main road is **Wooperton.** Anne Walton took the opportunity to start the **Roseden Farm Shop** at Wooperton after her family had grown up and developed interests of their own. Today it is a successful business where most of the wholesome produce is farm-reared and home-prepared, and Anne has acquired a reputation for good quality and presentation. As well as meat and meat by-products, other farm produce, homemade preserves, baking and confectionary, the shop also stocks a fine selection of local crafts.

The shop is only one of the farm's attractions. Also available are 10 ponies for trekking across some of the 800 acres of farmland which lies in the rolling foothills of the Cheviots on the edge of Glendale. A welcome at the end of such activity may be enjoyed in the popular coffee shop in very pleasant surroundings.

For visitors who wish to spend a while here, there is a self-catering cottage on the farm, although Anne will provide evening meals and Sunday lunch to order. However, the cottage is very popular with holidaymakers so, to avoid disappointment, it is advisable to book well in advance.

Roseden Farm Shop

The 15th century Percy's Cross, which stands by the roadside to the south of the village, commemorates the Battle of Hedgeley Moor, when a Lancastrian army was defeated by the Yorkists on 25th April 1464 during the Wars of the Roses. Two stones stand near by, about 10 yards apart; known as Percy's Leap, they are said to mark the distance leaped by Sir Ralph Percy's horse when the Earl was killed during the battle.

The Northumberland Coast

Seaton Delaval Hall

CHAPTER EIGHT

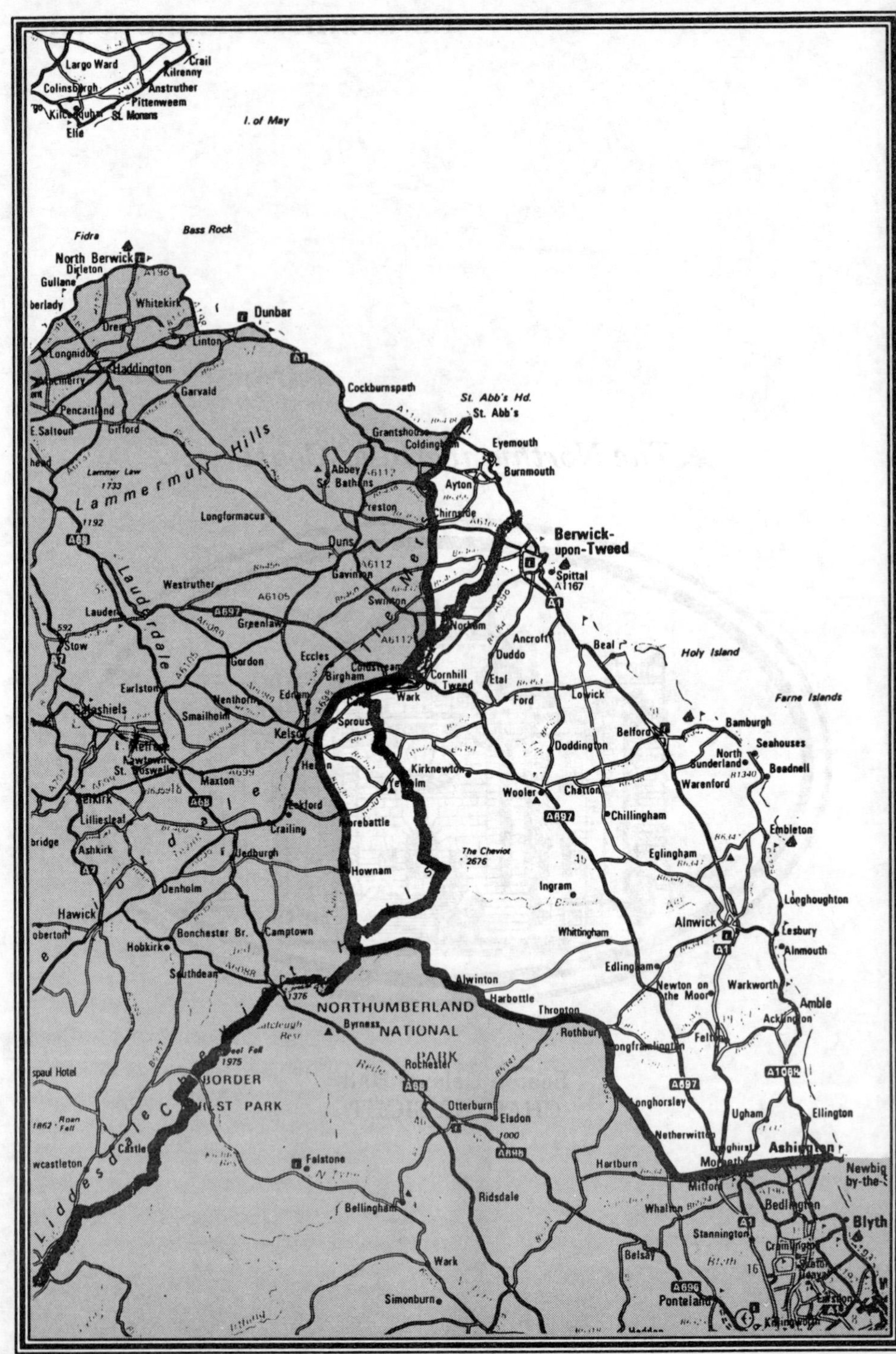
Largo Ward
Crail
Kilrenny
Colinsburgh
Anstruther
Pittenweem
St. Monans
Elie
I. of May
Fidra
Bass Rock
North Berwick
Dirleton
Gullane
Whitekirk
Dunbar
Linton
Haddington
Garvald
Cockburnspath
St. Abb's Hd.
St. Abb's
Pencaitland
Gifford
E.Saltoun
Grantshouse
Eyemouth
Burnmouth
Lammer Law
1733
Lammermuir Hills
Abbey St. Bathans
A6112
Ayton
Preston
Chirnside
Longformacus
1192
A68
Berwick-
upon-Tweed
Spittal
A1167
Duns
Lauderdale
Westruther
A6112
Gavinton
A6105
Swinton
The Merse
Lauder
A697
Greenlaw
A6112
Stow
Gordon
Eccles
Ancroft
Beal
Holy Island
Duddo
Birgham
Coldstream
Cornhill
on Tweed
Etal
Earlston
Ednam
Wark
Ford
Lowick
Farne Islands
Galashiels
Smailholm
Kelso
Sprouston
Bamburgh
Belford
Seahouses
North
Sunderland
Doddington
Beadnell
Melrose
St. Boswells
Maxton
Kirknewton
B1340
Yetholm
Wooler
Chatton
Warenford
A68
Selkirk
Lilliesleaf
Eckford
Morebattle
Crailing
A697
Chillingham
Embleton
Ashkirk
Jedburgh
The Cheviot
2676
Eglingham
A7
Hownam
Ingram
Denholm
Longhoughton
Hawick
Alnwick
Whittingham
Lesbury
Bonchester Br.
Camptown
A1
Alnmouth
Hobkirk
Southdean
Edlingham
Alwinton
Newton on
the Moor
Warkworth
Harbottle
NORTHUMBERLAND
NATIONAL
PARK
Amble
Byrness
Thropton
Acklington
Rothbury
Longframlington
Felton
1975
Rochester
BORDER
FOREST PARK
A68
A697
A1068
Otterburn
Longhorsley
Ugham
Ellington
Elsdon
1000
Netherwitton
A696
Ashington
Castle
Falstone
Hartburn
Morpeth
Mitford
Bellingham
Ridsdale
Whalton
Bedlington
Blyth
Stannington
A1
Liddesdale
Belsay
Wark
A696
Ponteland
Simonburn

Chapter Eight - Map Reference Guide
The Northumberland Coast

The Olde Ship Hotel - Seahouses

Beach House Hotel - Seahouses

Northumbria Crafts - Seahouses

The Links Hotel - Seahouses

The Norselands Gallery - Warenford

Warkworth House Hotel - Warkworth

North Cottage - Warkworth

Borgias - Bedlington

Dunstan Hill Farm Cottages - Embleton

Gianni's Pizzeria - Morpeth

The Copper Kettle - Bamburgh

Lakeside Hotel - Woodham

The Oaks Hotel - Alnwick

Bamburgh Castle Hotel - Seahouses

Warkworth Castle

CHAPTER EIGHT

The Northumberland Coast

Northumberland has one of the most romantically beautiful coasts in all England, much of it totally unspoilt, with great medieval castles, fishing villages and stretches of quiet beach of great loveliness.

Yet it has its contrasts too. The south-east corner of the county, between Blyth and Newbiggin, has an industrial history mainly of intensive mining along the great Northumberland coalfield. This is an industry which has declined rapidly in recent years, a loss from which the area is only slowly recovering. But even this industrialised part of Northumberland has much for the discerning visitor to enjoy.

Blyth claims its own piece of railway history with one of the earliest waggonways, dating from the 17th century and built to carry coal from the pits to the riverside. But the town really dates from the 18th century as a coastal port and shipbuilding centre with a lighthouse, built in 1788, in its centre. There are still sandy beaches, one extending down to Seaton Sluice, the other to the north, reached by a little ferry across the River Blyth.

A few miles inland from Seaton Sluice is what is widely regarded as being one of the finest houses in the north of England, Seaton Delaval Hall. This superb Vanbrugh mansion, the ancestral home of the Delavals, was built in the Palladian style in the early 18th century, and although the building suffered from a series of damaging fires, extensive restoration has been carried out.

Bedlington is an even older town than Blyth, and was formerly known as the county town of Bedlingtonshire, a district of County Durham until incorporated into Northumberland in 1844. It became the centre of a prosperous mining and iron-founding community and has two important links with railway history. It was the town in which the rolled-iron rails for the Stockton and Darlington Railway were manufactured and also the birthplace of the great locomotive engineer, Sir Daniel Gooch, disciple of Brunel and one of the greatest engineers of his day. The town also gave its name to a breed of dog, the Bedlington Terrier. There is an attractive country park at Humford Mill with an Information Centre, nature trails and horse-riding facilities. At Plessey Woods, south-west of the town, another country park extends along the wooded banks of the River Blyth, around Plessey Mill, with trails and a Visitor Centre.

On the side of an old listed building in a typically English street, an unobtrusive sign stands out because of its name - **'Borgias'**. And so it should, for this is one of Bedlington's finest restaurants, specialising in Greek and Italian cuisine as well as offering a choice in English cooking.

Socrates and Val Giazitzoglu have brought warm Greek hospitality to Bedlington and give all their customers their personal attention. Many of the dishes on the menu are local to their native island - 17 'house specialities' include 'Lamb Kebab Acropolis', 'Veal Corsica' and 'Pork Kebab Mytilene' - the last celebrating the capital of the island of Lesbos. Socrates and Val are very particular about using fresh and quality produce: large mussels, destined to be cooked in herbs and garlic, arrive from New Zealand! A 'Starters' list of 20 includes squid and frogs' legs.

Borgias

While savouring the extensive and adventurous menu, guests will be charmed by the original and creative decor. In the cosy intimacy of a candle-lit, cottage-style interior, a beautiful oriental rug hangs on the wall, and Mediterranean brass, copper and silverware from exposed beams. A striking feature is an area of stylish tile work in part of the ceiling.

Ashington is a sprawling village around the River Wansbeck, built to serve the mining industry, and now has modern shopping centres, swimming baths and leisure centres. The two-mile-long Wansbeck Riverside Park, which has been developed along the embankment, offers walking, sailing and angling facilities.

At **Woodhorn**, close to Ashington, there is a fascinating late-Anglo-Saxon church with a 13th century effigy of Agnes de Velence, wife of Hugh de Baliol, and a small museum and exhibition centre contains fragments of Saxon cross shafts. The Woodhorn Museum of the Mining Industry is being developed near by.

The **Lakeside Hotel** can be located close to the end of the A189 Spine road. It is conveniently situated only a short drive away from Newcastle upon Tyne with its busy international airport, and the beautiful coastline of Northumberland. It is surrounded by newly planted woodland, lakeside paths and picnic areas in Northumberland's attractive Queen Elizabeth II Country Park near the village of Woodhorn.

The Lakeside Hotel has succeeded in becoming the ideal venue for business and pleasure. It maintains a stylish, traditional atmosphere and manages to complement this with modern facilities to ensure that it is your first choice for meeting both friends and business colleagues and to sample both fine foods and wines with the most efficient service.

Every effort has been made to make your stay as special and as pleasurable as possible. As an overnight guest of the hotel, you can choose from 20 twin or double bedrooms, all with en-suite facilities. A host of other luxury items are at hand, including four poster beds, remote control television, radio, direct dial telephone, tea and coffee facilities and 24-hour room service.

The Trim Inn is a must for all you health fanatics. This is a professionally managed private health club offering use of an indoor heated swimming pool, spa bath, gymnasium including all the latest in fitness equipment, sunbed, sauna and even sailboard hire for those particularly energetic wind-surfers amongst you. Non-residents are also able to make use of the club's superb facilities by gaining membership, with special family rates being available.

In addition to comfort and numerous facilities, the Lakeside Hotel also offers excellent cuisine. There is an extensive a la carte and table d'hote menu, which includes mouthwatering dishes such as plump chicken breast stuffed with Camembert cheese sauce. Sunday dinners cater for all tastes and special business lunches are laid on by prior arrangement. These are both delicious and reasonably priced; whole rainbow trout pan-fried with lemon and prawns is one particularly appealing dish featured on the menu.

The executive chef is an expert in catering for special occasions such as wedding receptions and dinner dances, where special menus may be the order of the day. Buffets are sometimes more desirable at business conferences, and the Lakeside is willing to adapt accordingly.

The Lakeside also prides itself on its ability to provide an ideal, relaxed environment for all business meetings; be it conferences, seminars or training sessions. The main functions suite is designed to seat up to 200 delegates theatre-style, and there is a special board room for small meetings. Essential equipment is provided, including flip charts, videos, overhead projectors, fax and photocopying facilities, and soft drinks and mineral water are always close at hand.

As a guest, businessman, resident or otherwise, you can enjoy fine food and wine, efficient service and extensive facilities against a picturesque background of lakeside scenery.

Lakeside Hotel

Newbiggin by the Sea is a fishing village and small resort enjoying an attractive stretch of coastline with rocky inlets and sandy beaches, now being much improved after the depradations of the coal industry. The church of St Bartholomew has a particularily interesting 13th century interior.

Morpeth, Northumberland's County Town, seems a long way from the mining villages further down the Wansbeck, in both spirit and appearance. The ruins of a Norman castle overlook what was essentially a medieval settlement but one which, because it was difficult to defend, suffered badly from the depradations of the Scots. Its prosperity as a market town only developed in the 18th and 19th centuries when it became an important centre for this part of Northumberland. This led to the development of the town with some handsome buildings, most notably the Town Hall built to designs by Vanbrugh, and a handsome bridge over the Wansbeck was designed by John Dobson of Newcastle at a point surveyed by Telford around 1830. The church of St Mary's dates from the 14th century and has a rare Jesse window. Collingwood House, in Oldgate, was the former home of Admiral Lord Collingwood, who commanded the British fleet at Trafalgar after Nelson's death.

Somewhere not to be missed in Morpeth, in the medieval Chantry building on Bridge Street, is the Morpeth Chantry Bagpipe Museum, devoted to the story of the Northumbrian bagpipes and the heritage of music they played - and which is still played.

Gianni's Pizzeria

Gianni's Pizzeria in Morpeth is a lively and colourful place. Before 1960, the building used to be a cinema and today plenty of pictures and posters, dramatic fans and flair make it a really exciting place to eat in true Italian style. Owner Antonio Ribeito, along with his partners Paul and Chuck, have made this a really popular eating house with the locals. A huge range of pizzas and pastas are on offer with something to suit every taste, and we were pleased to note that lunch has a fixed charge with no hidden extras. There is also an extensive wine list and the three partners put a lot of energy into making people feel happy and well catered for. Paul, who is Head Chef, will happily serve English food (if you dare to ask!) and there is a fabulous range of starters and desserts to accompany your main meal. When in Rome, do as the Romans do - so when in Morpeth do as the 'Morpethians' do and eat at this happy pizzeria! And remember that in true Italian style, children are most welcome here, so you can start educating their tastebuds at an early age!

The coast and its hinterland, north of Morpeth and Ashington, is much more rural with quieter roads. Beyond the industrial villages of Lynemouth and Ellington is Cresswell with a 14th century fortified tower. It is possible to walk the coastal footpath past Druridge Bay to Amble, passing through the new Druridge Bay Country Park.

Amble is a small port on the mouth of the River Coquet, once important for the export of coal, but now enjoying new prosperity as a marina and sea-fishing centre, with a carefully restored harbour.

Just a mile offshore lies Coquet Island which, in Anglo-Saxon times, had a monastic foundation known as Cocwadae, and a Benedictine settlement of which only fragments of the foundations remain. The island had a bad reputation in former times for causing shipwrecks but is now a celebrated bird sanctuary, noted for colonies of terns, puffins and eider ducks. Managed by the Royal Society for the Protection of Birds, the island can be visited by boat from Amble on pre-arranged trips - the Tourist Information Centre in Amble will supply you with the details.

A short way north of Amble lies **Warkworth**, the first of the grand castles that so distinguish this coast. Magnificently situated above a wooded valley, this impressive fortress, with its soaring towers, dates back to a Norman Motte and Bailey castle built by Robert de Mowbray, Earl of Northumberland. It continued to be enlarged over the next few centuries, including the building of the great Carrickfergus Tower by Robert Fitz-Roger at the end of the 12th century. It came into the ownership of the Percys in 1331, in whose ownership it remained until comparatively recent times.

History was created here in 1399 when the Percys proclaimed Henry Bolingbroke, Henry IV, from these castle walls, an event immortalised in Shakespeare's play. Earlier history links it with Robert the Bruce and, before that, with the Venerable Bede and the Abbot of Holy Island as long ago as 737AD. In relatively recent years (if 1557 can be described as 'recent') the eighth Earl became involved in the Gunpowder Plot and died in the Tower.

Unusual and exciting is the walk to the hermitage along the riverside footpath below the castle, where a ferry takes you across the river to visit the tiny chapel hewn out of the solid rock. It dates from medieval times and was in use until late in the 16th century.

Warkworth is an interesting and beautiful village in its own right. An imposing fortified gatehouse on the 14th century bridge, now only used by pedestrians, would enable an invading army to be kept at bay north of the Coquet. If you want to understand why such a defence was required, you need look no further than the church of St Lawrence, which dates back to the 13th century and has a grim side to its history. The present building dates from Norman times and replaces an earlier Anglo-Saxon church. But it was here, in 1174, that 300 of the town's inhabitants, who had sought refuge from Scottish raiders, were brutally put to death by Duncan, Earl of Fife.

Such associations seem remote from the undisturbed tranquillity of the present building. Particularly worth seeing are the rare 14th century stone spire on the 13th century tower, some beautiful altar rails, examples of unusual Celtic crosses, the 90ft-long nave (the longest Norman nave in Northumberland) and a little room above the porch, called the Parvise, where local children were taught to read and write.

Whether travelling to Edinburgh or exploring Kielder Water and the Northumberland National Park, Warkworth is well worth visiting; and with numerous castles and places of historic interest along the coastline near by, visitors will find it a rewarding place to stay overnight and especially for a holiday.

The village remains virtually unspoilt by modern day transformations, as Joan and Duncan Oliver at the **Warkworth House Hotel** point out. The same can be said of their hotel. Just a short walk from the castle, it was built in 1830 and is a most impressive building. The exterior of the main house is typically Georgian with the windows on all three storeys symmetrically arranged. Inside, there is a magnificent staircase and arched window. The staircase originated from Brandenburgh House, the London residence of Queen Caroline, the estranged wife of George IV.

The hotel has recently re-opened after extensive modernisation. Joan and Duncan have been careful to ensure that this is in keeping with the period of the hotel. Each of the 14 bedrooms has been individually designed so that present-day luxuries enhance but do not intrude. Pre-dinner drinks in the bar or the lounge enable visitors to chat with locals, and perhaps gain 'inside' information on more 'hidden places' to visit. For those who like to try local flavour in the more literal sense, the Eden Restaurant offers a selection of speciality Northumbrian dishes on both the table d'hote and the a la carte menus.

Warkworth House Hotel

We found **North Cottage** on the outskirts of Warkworth at **Birling**. Edith and John Howliston provide first-rate bed and breakfast facilities at the cottage, which is around 300 years old. We thought it was a nice touch that visitors are treated to an afternoon tea on the day of arrival, courtesy of the owners. The ample breakfasts will set you up for the day before you set off to explore this lovely part of Northumberland, and at night you can enjoy a cup of tea with homemade cakes and biscuits.

The guest rooms are all comfortable and well furnished, with tea making facilities, electric blankets, clock radios and colour television. The double room and twin-bedded room are en-suite and there is a separate toilet and bathroom with bath and shower for the use of guests staying in the other rooms. In addition to the accommodation at the house, there is a field behind the cottage with room for five caravans or tent pitches. There are hot showers and toilet facilities here and the views are magnificent as the beach is less than 15 minutes walk away.

North Cottage

Alnmouth is a small resort with fine sands and a golf course, visible from the express trains of the East Coast main line that pass by at high speed. The village dates back to the 8th century and it was established as a port by William de Vesci. It is also the starting point of excellent walks along superb stretches of coastline either southwards, past extensive dunes to Warkworth, or north to the former fishing village of Boulmer.

Alnwick, just a short distance inland, is one of the most impressive towns of Northumbria, dominated as it is by the magnificent castle which was the stronghold of the great Percy dynasty from 1309 to the middle of the 18th century. It still has the feel and appearance of a great medieval military and commercial centre, being an important market town since the granting of its charter in 1291.

The castle began, like most of the Northumberland castles, as a Norman Motte and Bailey structure which was replaced in the 12th century by a circular stone keep, much added-to over the centuries. It was extensively rebuilt and restored in the 1850s and 60s by the Victorian architect, Anthony Salvin, for a later duke who sought to recapture the medieval feel of the castle whilst transforming it into a great country house with all the modern comforts of its time.

A number of rooms are open to the public and amongst its treasures are paintings by Titian, Tintoretto, Canaletto and Van Dyck, collections of Meissen china and superb furniture. There is also an extremely important archaeological museum and extensive archive collections, as well as the Royal Northumberland Fusiliers Regimental Museum in The Abbot's Tower.

Permits can be obtained to walk into adjacent Hulne Park, landscaped by the great (and Northumbrian-born) 'Capability' Brown, with the ruins of Hulne Priory, an early Carmelite foundation dating from 1240, and a gazebo believed to be designed by Robert Adam.

Alnwick town itself richly repays exploration, with narrow streets with such evocative names as Hotspur Gate (a surviving part of the town's 15th century fortifications and built by the Second Earl of Northumberland), Fenkle Street, Green Batt, Bondgate Without and Bondgate Within, a Market Place and several old coaching inns. The popular and colourful Alnwick Fair, dating from the 13th century, takes place each June or July; market day is Saturday.

The Oaks Hotel in Alnwick is an ideal stop-over point for visitors to Northumberland and is perfect for business people and holidaymakers alike.

Originally an 18th century Toll and Post House, this beautiful old building has recently undergone extensive conversion and refurbishment. You will find that what the Oaks offers now is a warm, friendly environment in which to unwind. Set in a quiet, residential area of Alnwick, the hotel is only several minutes walk from the town centre and just a quarter of a mile away from the A1.

All rooms have full en-suite facilities, plus direct dial telephones, clock radios, hairdryers, mini/fridge bars, remote control colour television, and tea and coffee making facilities.

Resident proprietors Middleton and Avril Dand can always be relied upon to provide a warm welcome. Enjoy a drink in the cosy cocktail bar, then sample lunch or a full a la carte dinner in the separate dining room. Home cooking is the order of the day here, using only the best of fresh local produce.

So, whether you are intending to push northwards, or simply to linger and explore these Northumbrian coastal borderlands, Alnwick and The Oaks Hotel is the perfect place for a break in your journey.

Craster is a small and unpretentious fishing village which is nationally famous for its oak-smoked kippers, cured in the village by a process which is still a well-kept secret. There is a shell museum in the village and a small Countryside Centre.

The Oaks Hotel

Craster is also the starting point for a superb short coastal walk to Dunstanburgh Castle, one of the most evocative castle ruins of all, superbly situated on a headland above the coast. It was built as a personal refuge, in 1313, by Thomas, Earl of Lancaster, one of the many powerful enemies of the ineffectual King Edward II. Having been badly damaged by a siege in 1464 during the Wars of the Roses, it has never really been repaired, its monumental and shattered gatehouse like a gigantic theatrical set turned reality.

This part of Northumberland, between Craster and Berwick, forms part of one of Britain's Areas of Outstanding Natural Beauty - the Northumberland Coast. In addition, it is also one of the nation's Heritage Coasts which, because of its great scenic beauty and natural history, requires careful protection and management measures. Much of the area, including the Farne Islands, is also owned by the National Trust, which gives additional protection. It is a wonderful area to explore on foot, leaving the car at a convenient car park or taking the coastal bus that links Berwick, Bamburgh and Alnwick, via most of the coastal villages.

Since Alnwick and its surroundings undoubtedly have a lot to offer, you will certainly want to explore the area thoroughly. Now, if what you are looking for is well-equipped self-catering accommodation in restful surroundings, then Mrs Morton at **Dunstan Hill Farm** has just the thing for you.

Situated between Craster and Embleton, you will see four stone-built cottages sitting on a country lane leading to the farm, and enjoying a picturesque view of Dunstanburgh Castle.

This is Dunstan Hill Farm cottages - all of which have colour TV, metered central heating and open fires. Visitors, however, should bring along their own sheets and pillowcases. Kitchenettes are fully equipped, with fuel and electricity charges all included in your tariff.

Surrounded by farm fields, and with a grassy play area of its own, Dunstan Hill Farm cottages are ideal for families and children. Mrs Morton will supply a cot and high chair should you require them - and if you let her know, she can also arrange for the supply and delivery of daily papers, groceries, milk and eggs.

Just one and a half miles from the coast, Dunstan Hill offers distant sea views, and the surrounding area is perfect for golfing, walking and birdwatching. As well as being an ideal base for visiting local places of interest such as Alnwick and Bamburgh Castles, you will find that these lovely cottages are ideally situated for exploring Northumbria and the Scottish borders.

Dunstan Hill Farm cottages

It is possible to continue a coastal walk from Dunstanburgh, around Embleton Bay, past Snook Point, to Low Newton, or to cross Embleton Links to the little village of Embleton, with its 14th century church and a vicarage which is partly a 14th century pele tower.

At **Low Newton-by-the-Sea**, land owned by the National Trust includes

Newton Pool, a freshwater lake which is a fascinating Nature Reserve, with such species as mute swan, teal, sedge-warbler, dabchick, goldeneye and pochard. Public access is permitted to the edge of the reserve and there are parking bays and hides. Newton Links is another area of rough grazing and dunes from where there are superb views of the coastline, with further walking opportunities past Beadnell Bay to Beadnell and on to Seahouses and Bamburgh.

Newton-by-the-Sea

At **Beadnell** there is a little harbour, and some important 18th century limekilns also owned by the National Trust. Running eastwards from the harbour into the sea is Ebb's Nook, a narrow strip of land where there are the remains of a 13th century chapel dedicated to St Ebba. She was the sister of King Oswald, King of Northumbria, and St Abb's Head, on the Berwickshire coast, is named after her.

This, again, is a delightful stretch of coast and you can follow the coastline either by shore path or along the B1340 past St Aidan's Dunes to Seahouses.

Seahouses is an active fishing port and small seaside resort, strategically situated to explore this part of the Heritage Coast, with a National Trust Shop and Information Centre. Here too, you will find an interesting harbour, magnificent beaches and sand dunes stretching for miles on either side of the town.

Seahouses

The Olde Ship Hotel in Seahouses is certainly aptly named. The saloon and cabin bars are wonderfully decorated with abundant displays of nautical pieces. There are ships' figure-heads dating from the 19th century, brass lamps, navigating instruments and old-time fishing artifacts. The sea-faring theme continues, in the compact dining-room and upstairs in the long gallery, through marine paintings and model ships.

However, in the 10 bedrooms the accent is quite definitely on 20th century comfort. Guests are well looked after and all tastes are catered for. The menu for the five-course dinner is changed every night and always includes a seafood dish and a vegetarian meal among its selection, as well as a tantalising choice of sweets. A popular lunch-time snack is one of the various tasty sandwiches served in the bar.

The Olde Ship Hotel started life in 1745 but not as a hotel: it was a farmhouse for 67 years before it first became licensed. Nowadays it has an excellent reputation for comfortable relaxation in old-fashioned surroundings. Mr and Mrs Glen, the owners, can offer plenty of information about the many interesting places to visit in the area, and even provide a courtesy coach to and from Chathill station.

The Olde Ship Hotel

Set midway between the beach and fishing harbour we found the **Beach House Hotel,** a two-star family run hotel with spectacular views of the offshore islands, Bamburgh Castle and the Cheviot Hills. The building was constructed in the 1920's, but has been much extended and improved over the past 15 years by the present owners, Mr and Mrs Craigs. There are now 14 bedrooms, each with en-suite bath or shower, colour television and many complimentary extras. There are 3 guest lounges, one with an open fire and a stunning view of the sea. Mr and Mrs Craigs provide the very best of traditional home cooking, making use of locally sourced fish, meat, fruit and vegetables. This friendly hotel recently won the 'Holiday Hosts" award organised by the local BBC radio station and Northumbrian Tourist Board, so the warmest of welcomes is guaranteed.

Beach House Hotel

When looking for a memento of your visit to Seahouses - or perhaps just an original and unusual gift for someone you know - we suggest you choose something from the high quality craftwork on offer at Northumbria Crafts.

The building which now houses this fascinating little craft shop was initially a ship's chandlers, and has been used in scenes from various television programmes.

Northumbria Crafts sits adjacent to the quay at Seahouses and here you will find items made by Northumbrian craft workers. In fact, all crafts for sale have a local material or labour element. What we found interesting is that not only can you buy the finished goods - you can also buy the component parts involved within the manufacturing process.

Proprietors John and Patricia Frisby offer a postal service and are willing to try to obtain unusual pieces for customers who are involved in producing their own crafts - perhaps bobbins for lace making, tatting shuttles, netting needles or hairpins, used to produce hairpin lace. Look over the selection of craft books for sale - and if you're looking for something in particular you can place an order for a non-stock title and take advantage of the postal service.

Drivers will find ample car parking space within 200 yards of the craft shop, and wheelchair users will have no difficulty entering as there are no steps.

Northumbria Crafts

Sitting in King Street, close to the beach and harbour, you will find **The Links Hotel.** Recently extensively refurbished, and personally run by Mrs Findlay, The Links offers impressive standards of accommodation to those of you intending to stay a while in this picturesque harbour town.

The Links Hotel

The hotel has 10 bedrooms, four with en-suite facilities and all with colour TV and tea and coffee making facilities. A relaxing cottage-style decor in the 40-cover restaurant makes it the ideal place for an intimate meal - and non-residents are welcome too.

Light meals in a traditional vein are served daily, as well as Sunday lunches.

Children are welcome at The Links, and Mrs Findlay operates a baby-listening service. With this in mind, you may like to enjoy a game of pool or darts after your meal. Failing that, you can simply retire to the bar and relax - which is, after all, why you came away in the first place!

The Bamburgh Castle Hotel of Seahouses looks over all three of Northumberland's main attractions; the Farne Islands, Holy Island and Bamburgh Castle. The Hotel has a large history; built in 1800, it has served multiple purposes, showing itself as a veterinary clinic, once holding school rooms, and even serving as a public house. One part of the building, which was at one time separate but is now an integral part of the Hotel, was a fire station! It now houses bedrooms, although the rooms each have a reminder of their past by going under names such as 'Watch Room'. Other bedrooms in the main building are named novelly after fishing boats which can be seen in the small harbour nearby.

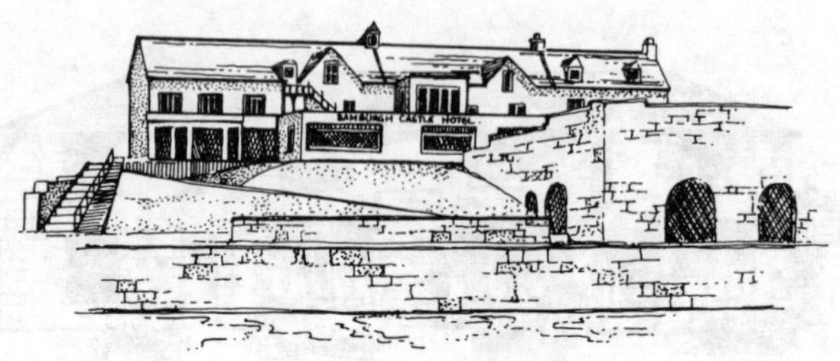

Bamburgh Castle Hotel

The Hotel has 20 bedrooms, all en-suite. These are very impressive, with choices that include the opportunity to have sea views, a four poster bed or a jacuzzi. Family rooms and cots for children under three are available, and pets, though not allowed in public areas, are permitted.

There are two lounges, one non-smoking, a separate public bar, and a resident's bar overlooking the coastline. Superb gardens surround the Hotel, and you would have to agree that the Bamburgh Castle Hotel has the best views around.

The Hotel provides its very own 'hospitality package', which includes complimentary sherry on arrival for guests, boxed soap, bubble bath and shampoo, tea and coffee facilities plus hot chocolate and biscuits, satellite TV, and use of exercise machines, putting green and golf driving net. Those staying a week receive an additional basket of fruit and mineral water in their bedroom on arrival. Children are not forgotten, each receiving a 'goodie bag' and a soft drink.

Paul and June Hopper who run the hotel are planning to upgrade the bedrooms even further in the future, and the results will be interesting to see judging by their innovative ideas and present high standard.

Apart from Seahouses itself and local attractions such as the castles at Alnwick, Bamburgh and Warkworth, nature lovers can enjoy a boat trip to the nearby Farne Islands. Sailings run from May to October in good weather. This small group of 28 uninhabited islands of volcanic Whin Sill rock, just off the coast at Bamburgh, provides a sanctuary for over 17 species of sea birds, including kittiwake, fulmar, eider-duck, puffin, guillemot and tern. It is also home for a large colony of grey seal.

The islands have important Christian links too, being the place, on **Inner Farne**, where St Cuthbert died in 687AD. His body was carried on a journey around Northumbria which continued for several centuries until a final resting place was found in Durham Cathedral. A little chapel was built here to his memory and restored in Victorian times. The nearby Tower House was built in medieval times by Prior Castell - according to tradition, on the site of Cuthbert's cell.

Landings are permitted on Inner Farne and Staple Island, though times are restricted for conservation reasons and advance booking is urged in the busy times of year. There are nature trails on both islands, as well as a small exhibition centre in the former chapel of St Mary on Inner Farne. The lighthouse, built in 1809, has Grace Darling associations.

Grace Darling (1815-42) was the celebrated Victorian heroine who, in 1838, rowed out with her father from the Longstone Lighthouse, in a ferocious storm, to rescue the survivors of the steam ship, 'Forfarshire', which had foundered on the Farne Island rocks. She died of tuberculosis only four years later, still only in her twenties, and is buried in Bamburgh churchyard. There is a suitably enshrined monument to her courage, positioned, it is said, so that it may be seen by mariners from ships at sea. The Grace Darling Museum, in Radcliffe Road in Bamburgh, contains memorabilia of the rescue of the 'Forfarshire'.

Bamburgh Castle is epic in scale, even by the standards of this coastline of spectacular castles. Situated on a dramatic outcrop of Whin Sill rock overlooking the sea, it was almost certainly the royal seat of the first Kings of Northumbria from the 6th century onwards. The dynasty was founded by the Saxon King Ida in 547AD and mentioned in the 'Anglo-Saxon Chronicle'. The present castle has a massive 12th century keep around which huge baileys were constructed. The castle was extensively rebuilt and restored in the 18th and 19th centuries, latterly by the first Lord Armstrong, whose family still own the building.

Open to the public, rooms on display include the Armoury, Grand King's Hall, Court Room, Keep Hall, Bakehouse and Victorian Scullery, with collections of tapestries, ceramics, furniture and paintings, and an exhibition about the first Lord Armstrong and his many remarkable engineering inventions.

A visit to Bamburgh would not be complete without sampling the homemade delights of the **Copper Kettle Tearooms**. With the exception of bread, the owners - David Bates and Rosemary Christie - do all their own baking on the premises.

It would be difficult to meet a couple as friendly as David and Rosemary, who were both assistant bank managers before buying the restaurant in 1988. The building itself dates back to the early 1700s and boasted a thatched roof until 1809 when it was slated. Formerly estate workers' cottages, the building is now listed.

This is a very popular eating place - not surprising when you consider the standard of service provided and the cost. The restaurant has seating room for over 50 people, and for fine, sunny days, the garden seats a further 12.

Open seven days a week during the summer months, David and Rosemary work with the assistance of eight part-time staff, providing an extensive menu which also caters for vegetarians. Do note, however, that no smoking is allowed inside the restaurant, although those who wish to can of course smoke in the garden.

Inside, you will see various local arts on display - much of this is for sale, so don't be afraid to ask if something catches your eye. A display cabinet shows off china and there are copper kettles and drinking pots hanging from the wooden beams. You can also treat yourself to some speciality confections - try the Copper Kettle's sweets, jams, cookies or honey.

On entering the vestibule, a display shows the original Copper Kettle which gave its name to this establishment, a restaurant now since the 1950s. The carved oak panelling depicts scenes of local interest.

The Copper Kettle is run with such a high level of enthusiasm and friendliness that it offers probably the best value for money in the area. It is certainly worth seeking out.

The Copper Kettle

Our last port of call for this chapter was at **Warenford**, just off the A1, some five miles south-west of Bamburgh. The Old School at Warenford now houses the **Norselands Gallery** and a ceramic workshop, Studio Two. Against the backdrop of the lovely glazed tiles of the original Victorian classroom are displayed a fine selection of drawings, paintings, prints and original crafts, all works of British artists. In their ceramic sculpture, Barrie and Veronica Rawlinson create, from research and observation, people, children, fantasy figures and natural objects familiar to us all. They are always pleased to discuss specially commissioned pieces.

The Norselands Gallery

Dunstanburgh Castle

Berwick & The Border

Cheviot Sheep

CHAPTER NINE

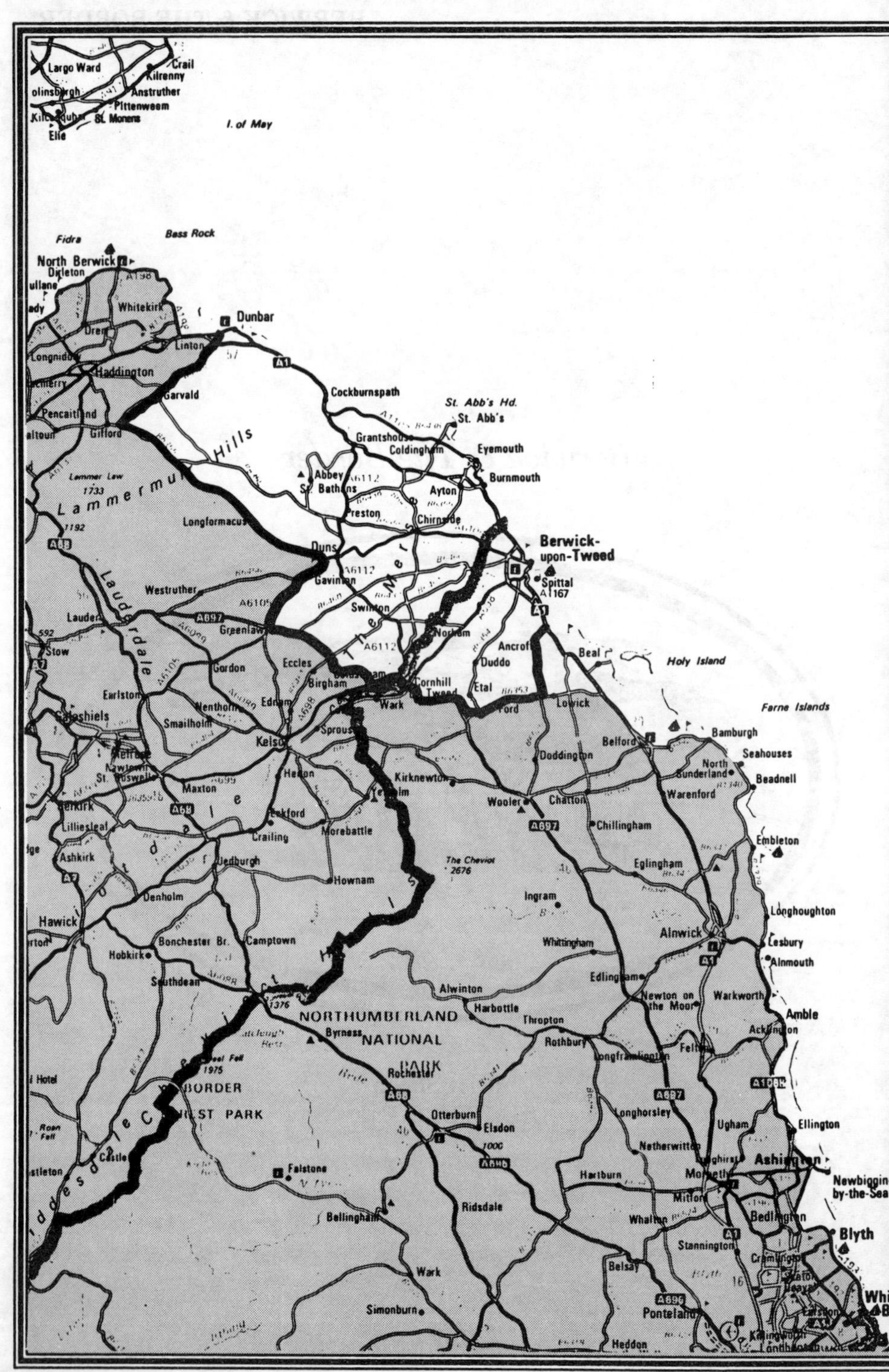

Largo Ward
Crail
Kilrenny
Anstruther
Pittenweem
St. Monans
Elie
I. of May
Fidra
Bass Rock
North Berwick
Dirleton
Whitekirk
Dunbar
Linton
Haddington
Garvald
Cockburnspath
St. Abb's Hd.
St. Abb's
Pencaitland
Gifford
Grantshouse
Coldingham
Eyemouth
Lammermuir Hills
Lammer Law
1733
Abbey St. Bathans
A6112
Burnmouth
Ayton
1192
Longformacus
Preston
Chirnside
Duns
Berwick-upon-Tweed
Spittal
Lauderdale
Westruther
Gavinton
The Merse
A6105
A1167
Swinton
Lauder
A697
Greenlaw
Norham
592
Stow
Ancroft
Beal
Holy Island
Gordon
Eccles
Duddo
Earlston
Birgham
Cornhill
Tweed
Wark
Etal
Ford
Lowick
Farne Islands
Nenthorn
Ednam
Smailholm
Kelso
Bamburgh
Belford
Seahouses
Doddington
North Sunderland
Beadnell
St. Boswells
Maxton
Hedon
Kirknewton
Yetholm
Wooler
Chatton
Warenford
A68
Eckford
Lilliesleaf
Crailing
Morebattle
A697
Chillingham
Embleton
Ashkirk
Jedburgh
The Cheviot
2676
Eglingham
Hownam
Denholm
Ingram
Longhoughton
Hawick
Alnwick
Lesbury
Bonchester Br.
Camptown
Whittingham
Hobkirk
Alnmouth
Southdean
Alwinton
Edlingham
Newton on the Moor
Warkworth
1376
Harbottle
Amble
NORTHUMBERLAND
Thropton
Acklington
Byrness
NATIONAL
Rothbury
PARK
Longframlington
1975
Rochester
Felton
BORDER
A697
A1068
Otterburn
Longhorsley
Elsdon
Ugham
Ellington
Castleton
Netherwitton
Falstone
Ashington
Hartburn
Morpeth
Newbiggin-by-the-Sea
Bellingham
Ridsdale
Mitford
Whalton
Bedlington
Blyth
Stannington
Cramlington
Belsay
Wark
Simonburn
A696
Ponteland
Heddon

Chapter Nine - Map Reference Guide
Berwick & The Border

Berwick Town Hall &
Berwick Borough Museum & Art Gallery - Berwick-upon-Tweed

Meadow House - Berwick-upon-Tweed

Belford Craft Gallery - Belford

Noel Bray Studio - Belford

Beachcomber Cottages - Goswick

The Rob Roy Seafood Restaurant - Tweedmouth

Loreto Guest House - Wooler

The Galleon - Spittal

North View Lodge - Holy Island

Manor House Hotel - Holy Island

Meadow Hill Guest House - Berwick-upon-Tweed

Waren House Hotel - Waren Mill

Red Lion Hotel - Wooler

Earle Hill Head Farm - Earle

Ladythorne House - Cheswick

Fishers Arms - Horncliffe

Tankerville Arms Hotel - Wooler

Middle Ord Farm - East Ord

Wild White Cattle at Chillingham

CHAPTER NINE

Berwick and the Border

The River Tweed forms, for much of its length, the boundary between two nations and two counties - England and Northumberland, Scotland and Berwickshire.

This leaves the ancient town of **Berwick** in a curiously ambiguous position. The heart of the old town lies across on the Scottish side of the boundary. Apart from its immediate hinterland, its natural territory named after the town - Berwickshire - lies in Scotland. Scots would argue that it is a tiny corner of Scotland claimed by England.

Little wonder it has been fought and quarrelled over for a thousand years and more. Little wonder that it has changed hands so many times as to make its inhabitants not entirely certain, even yet, where their true allegiance lies.

It was, for example, given by William the Lion of Scotland to the English Crown in 1147 as part of his ransom after he had been captured at Alnwick. Richard the Lionheart had to concede it to Scotland to raise money to pay for his crusades and the town continued to change hands until 1482 when it was finally confirmed as being part of England.

Even then, for a time, Berwick became almost a country in itself, an independent 'free town' which had to be specifically mentioned in Acts of Parliament until 1746. To confuse the issue a little more, Berwick had its status as a Scottish Burgh, lost in 1368, restored by Lord Lyon in 1958. This makes it now a town which technically belongs to both nations - surely the happiest compromise!

It is linked with Northumberland by three bridges across the Tweed; the Royal Tweed Bridge carring the A1, Berwick Bridge, a handsome stone bridge with 15 arches dating from 1624, and the enormous 126ft-high Royal Border Bridge carrying the East Coast main-line railway, built in 1847 by Robert Stephenson.

What makes Berwick unique, apart from its status, is its extensive fortifications, ordered by Elizabeth I to replace part of the earlier town wall. They were built in 1558 by Italian engineers, who were experts at creating defences to exploit the full use of artillery to defend the town. The huge grassy ramparts still have an uncannily modern appearance. A gun tower and part of the west wall are open to the public.

Berwick's original medieval walls can still be walked, and the old townscape within the walls is a colourful blend of warm sandstone and red pantiles. There are fine buildings, many of them Georgian, including the neo-Classical Town Hall and the Ravensdowne Barracks, designed by Vanbrugh and built between 1717 and 1721. They were reputed to be the first barracks ever built, as a result of complaints by local people about having to constantly billet soldiers. The barracks now house the King's Own Scottish Borderers' Regimental Museum.

The Berwick skyline is dominated by the imposing Town Hall with its clock, octagonal cupola and spire rising 150ft to the top of its weather-vane. Rebuilt in 1754, this fine building has a facade as elaborate as its well-documented history.

Berwick Town Hall

On the ground floor, markets were held in the Exchange. Shops and cells existed where now a gift shop and coffee house stand. Summertime guided tours enable visitors to explore the upper storeys containing civic rooms, the bell chamber and the town gaol (which provides a chastening glimpse of the past). This comprises the debtors' prison (now holding the Cell Block Museum) and adjoining felons' cells. The sloping wooden bed in the drunkards' cell raises fleeting smiles, soon erased by the condemned cell and a grim display of gaolers' tools of trade. However, the neighbouring bell chamber has a charming history and visitors are sometimes allowed to ring the eight named bells. Each one had its own function: 'Cuthbert', for instance, was rung only on Shrove Tuesday.

Facing the Holy Trinity Parish Church, the main entrance to the Barracks (built in 1721) leads through the barracks square to the Clock Block. Here the **Berwick Borough Museum and Art Gallery** invites visitors to peer through a Window on Berwick, enter the dragon and step into a Cairo bazaar. Sir William Burrell donated one tenth of his collection of art treasures to the museum, a total of some 800 pieces. There are 46 important paintings including a Degas and many fine items of porcelain, glass and metalware.

Berwick Borough Museum and Art Gallery

Originally built as the Mayor's out-of-town house, **Meadow House,** on the A1 north of Berwick, is now a popular public house and restaurant offering a large and varied menu of bar snacks, three-course lunches and suppers. Michael and Edith Hearn have put together an interesting selection, to suit all tastes, in each of the courses, which range from simple dishes to something richer. Specialities include seafood platter and crab salad, in season, and generous portions of steaks cooked in at least four different delicious ways. There is also plenty of choice for vegetarians. The wine list offers at least 27 different labels and then, to finish with, coffee made with a spirit or liqueur.

The private house is in the oldest part of the building, which dates back to 1861, and all rooms face south, since the north-facing wall is listed as having no windows. Real and traditional beer ensures a strong local trade. Berwick has exchanged borders with Scotland and England as many as 13 times but, for the moment at least, Meadow House can rightfully boast of being 'the first and last public house in England'.

Meadow House

Situated just outside Berwick on Duns Road, the **Meadow Hill Guest House** enjoys superb views of the Tweed Valley, the Cheviot Hills and the spectacular Border countryside. Although reputed to stand on the burial grounds of the infamous 14th century Battle of Halidon Hill, guests are assured of a peaceful time here.

Albert and Jennifer Whyte are registered with the English Tourist Board and offer their guests a choice of comfortable and well-equipped rooms, two being ideally suited to families. An added luxury is the use of a sauna! Children are specially catered for and dogs are permitted by prior reservation. For guests arriving by train, a courtesy car is available from the railway station.

Full English Breakfast is included with accommodation, and in the evening guests may choose to dine in and enjoy traditional home cooking, or eat out at a selection of recommended local places. Meadow Hill also has a table license and lounge bar for the convenience of residents.

Meadow Hill Guest House

Tweedmouth, on the 'English' side of the Tweed, is mainly a suburb of Berwick, but near the War Memorial is still to be found the ancient 'Louping Stone', over which newly-weds are supposed to leap to bring them luck and prosperity.

On the corner of Dock Road and Lees Lane is **The Rob Roy Seafood Restaurant,** owned and run by Keith and Julie Wilson. Mr Wilson was trained in France and he and his chefs favour traditional French recipes using delicate wines for poaching and for sauces. Indeed, the Rob Roy has an intriguing list of specialist wines and Mr Wilson will be happy to advise patrons on a choice to complement their meal.

All the fish is bought direct from local fishermen at Berwick, Seahouses or Eyemouth and is personally chosen and prepared by Mr Wilson, and the menus, which are changed every 4 to 6 weeks, reflect the fish, seafood and game that are in season. Particular dishes for which the Rob Roy is well known include a delicious seafood platter consisting of lobster, smoked salmon, mussels and prawns served with an asparagus salad and saute potatoes; Salmon Limoux - Tweed salmon poached in sparkling French wine and cream; Duckling Cassis - breast of duckling cooked and served in blackcurrant liqueur sauce; and prime rump steak cooked with onion and mushrooms and served in a sauce of whisky and cream. There is plenty here for the discerning diner!

One unique feature of the Rob Roy is the Salmon Co. Bar, where the bar has been constructed entirely from fish boxes belonging to the Berwick Salmon Fisheries Company. The restaurant has recently been named Local Seafood Pub 91 by the Seafish Industries Authority, and it may also interest you to know that they offer bed and breakfast accommodation - handy after an evening of over-indulgence, perhaps!

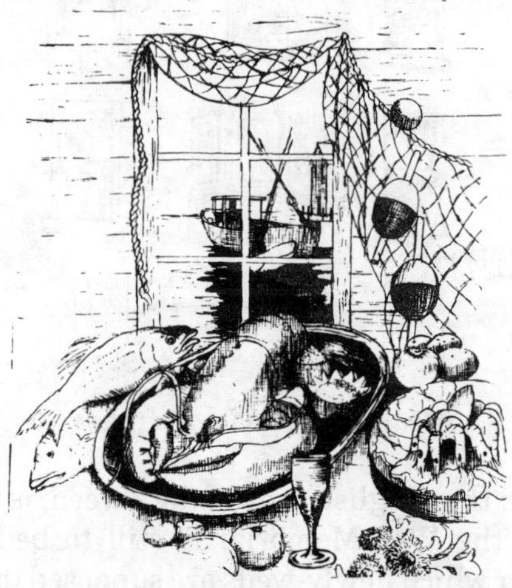

The Rob Roy Seafood Restaurant

Spittal, on the south of the Tweed estuary, has extensive sands and serves as the main holiday resort for Berwick, with a promenade, lifeboat station and a variety of seaside attractions.

The Galleon in Spittal was once two terrace houses and a bakery, which have been converted into a licensed inn and restaurant. The extensive refurbishment has resulted in a charming and homely atmosphere where all guests will receive a warm welcome and the personal attention of their host, Christine Mooney. Parts of the building are almost 200 years old, which may help explain the odd appearances of two elderly regulars - ghosts - who have been seen, separately, at the rear of the pub, from time to time. Christine doesn't know who they are. They're not unfriendly, apparently, but they do move things around and switch things on and off.

The menus in the bars and restaurant offer a range of quality, traditional home-cooked food. There is always much more of a choice of fresh fish dishes at coastal resorts, and the menu here reflects this. The portions are all very generous, so children's menus are also available. As walkers will find, the inn is a convenient place to stop for refreshment and the Galleon is also a popular meeting place for locals.

The Galleon

If you have ever been interested in farming life, then **Middle Ord House,** an attractive Georgian residence built in 1783, is a good choice for a relaxed short stay or holiday.

The farm can be located three miles from Berwick along the A698 and one mile from **East Ord** village. It is positioned on 550 acres of working farmland, surrounded by woodland and walled gardens. Visitors are invited to wander around the grounds and observe the various animals, as all-day access is offered.

On entering this impressive farmhouse, Joan Gray will welcome you most warmly before showing you the delightful bedrooms, which include one double and two twin, en-suite facilities and even a four poster bed if desired. Tea and coffee facilities can be found in all the bedrooms.

You can watch TV in a very well-appointed lounge (non-smoking) and anyone wishing to smoke can do so in the reading/smoker's lounge which features a beautiful original fireplace of note. A full and comprehensive English breakfast is served in the gracious dining room.

Self-catering (four-bedroomed) accommodation is also available on the farm.

Middle Ord Farm

Four miles upriver from Berwick and a mile north of the A698 Kelso road, lies the untouched riverside village of **Horncliffe**. To reach the village, drive down the short cul-de-sac which ends on the southern bank of the River Tweed. Not far away you'll find the **Fishers Arms**, a fine 200-year-old pub run by local Andrew Miller and his wife, Andrea. The pub is popular with locals and visitors alike. Andrew and Andrea pride themselves on serving good beer and providing their customers with a varied selection of meals and bar snacks, which are available at all times at reasonable prices. After visiting the pub, we suggest a riverside walk which will lead you to a most interseting suspension bridge. Here, the River Tweed forms the border between England and Scotland. Expect to see salmon fishing from both banks. For those of you looking for overnight accommodation, the

Fishers Arms has two twin and one single room available.

Fishers Arms

The River Tweed is famous for both salmon and swans, and Tweeddale, more than any part of the two kingdoms, epitomises Border Country - a region of soft beauty and gentle grandeur. It is, inevitably, tinged by a sadness as if even the passing centuries have not entirely cleaned the memory of bitter strife and bloodshed from the constant border wars, skirmishes and raids. Towns and villages outside the safety of Berwick's walls are noticeably smaller and plainer than such a fertile landscape would suggest is possible. Churches are austere, and were often used for defence as well as worship, farmhouses fortified, and communities scattered as if even to this very day recollections linger.

Nowhere is this sense of sadness stronger than at Flodden Field, only a short drive south-west from Berwick, past the village of **Duddo**, which, even now, has its Tudor look-out tower; and **Etal**, a particularly pretty estate village with thatched cottages. Here you'll see the ruins of a 14th century castle, destroyed by King James IV on his way to Flodden. Not far beyond Branxton, reached off the Coldstream road (A697), lies the battleground where, in 1513, James IV's massive army marched south across the border. He made his headquarters at Ford Castle, which also survives, though in much altered form.

On 9th September 1513 - 'Black Friday' - an English army, under the

Earl of Surrey, faced James's army on Branxton Hill. The King was outmanoeuvred and died bravely along with 9,000 of his men, his body being brought to Branxton's 12th century church before being carried on to Berwick; the English, too, lost 5,000 men. The Scottish lament, 'The Flowers of the Forest', was written to commemorate this tragic event. Every year, in August, as part of Coldstream Civic week, a procession is made to lay a wreath at the simple granite memorial cross in Flodden Field and to hear the lament played by pipes.

At **Norham**, on the Tweed just south of Horncliffe, is another of the castles which James destroyed on the way to his fateful encounter at Flodden. This was owned by the Prince Bishops of Durham and, until that time, had a reputation for being impregnable. But it was rebuilt in the later 16th century and remains an impressive example of a castle of its period. Norham village, too, is rich in interest. It was here that St Aidan crossed the Tweed in 635AD on his journey from Iona, West Scotland, to Lindisfarne, and the village has a large Norman church, appropriately dedicated to St Cuthbert.

It is in Norham that an unusual ceremony takes place which has long Christian and perhaps even pre-Christian associations - the Blessing of the Nets - held at midnight every 13th February to mark the beginning of the salmon fishing season.

If you head south on the A697 from **Branxton**, you will eventually come to the little market town of Wooler. Standing on the northern edge of the Cheviots, Wooler has a simplicity and purposefulness even to this day, which again indicates that this was an area which never enjoyed the prosperity of less troubled regions. Many cattle fairs, however, took place here, and it is an excellent centre for exploring both the Cheviots and the border country.

There are superb walking opportunities from the very edge of the town - for example, onto **Wooler** hillfort immediately west of the town, an Iron Age hillfort and an impressive viewpoint, or continuing to Earle Whin and Wooler Common or via Harthope onto The Cheviot itself. Alternatively, you can take a vehicle into the Harthope Valley with a choice of walks, easy or strenuous, up and through the magnificent hillsides of this part of the Northumberland National Park.

If you decide to use Wooler as your holiday base, you will find no shortage of good accommodation in and around the town.

The Red Lion Hotel is over 300 years old - and is still well worth a visit! Dating back to 1671, this listed building is one of the oldest inns in Northumberland. Originally standing two storeys high, a third storey was added at the turn of the century.

Until 1979 the public right of way came through the centre of the Hotel - needless to say, this is no longer the case!

This cosy hotel has a real old world charm with solid stone walls, exposed wood beams and a real coal fire. You can always expect a warm welcome from resident proprietors Mr and Mrs Whaley, who can offer bar snacks and lunches as well as a full a la carte evening menu.

Should you decide to linger and enjoy an overnight stay at the Red Lion, there are seven bedrooms, four with en-suite facilities, and all with TV and tea making facilities.

You may not have a horse to hitch up in the Hotel's stables, but there are ample car parking facilities. The Red Lion is open all year long, seven days a week - and local readers will want to note that Mr Whaley has a function room at the rear of the Hotel which can accommodate parties of up to 80.

Red Lion Hotel

Wooler stands midway between Newcastle and Edinburgh, and in the 18th and early-19th centuries, it became an important halt on the main North-South coaching route. In 1841, the journey from London to Edinburgh was drastically reduced to just 44 hours, including stops. One legacy of this era is the **Tankerville Arms Hotel**, originally a 17th century coaching inn and now an elegant family-run hotel. In recent years, extensive modernisation has been carried out to this Grade I listed building, though care has been taken to maintain its historic appearance. The two-star hotel has 16 bedrooms, most with a scenic view over open fields, en-suite bathroom, colour television and tea making facilities. There is also a choice of bars, a beer garden with children's play area, and an excellent restaurant and bistro serving the very best of Northumbrian fare. Look out for a broad stone building on the edge of town, partially hidden behind masses of Virginia creeper.

Tankerville Arms Hotel

Loreto Guest House in Wooler is well situated for walking and touring in the Northumberland National Park and the Cheviots. Set in landscaped grounds, this elegant Georgian house enjoys Grade I listing, while the quality of accommodation offered by Mrs Allan merits a two-crown rating.

Five of the seven bedrooms are en-suite - including the two on the ground floor which cater for the needs of disabled visitors - and there is a licensed restaurant.

The tasteful decor and furnishings enhance the character of the house, but guests are sure to find the numerous wildlife trophies intriguing. In the large games room there are two full-sized snooker tables, so it may come as no surprise to learn that guests at the Loreto have included the snooker stars John Virgo and Dennis Taylor!

Loreto Guest House

Two miles to the south-west of Wooler, we went in search of the Earle Hill Household and Farming Museum. This really is a hidden place. Take 'Cheviot Street' towards the hamlet of Middleton, fork right after a mile, then turn right in **Earle** and follow the road to the end. Your journey will, however, be well rewarded. Mrs Sylvia Armstrong has been collecting for her charming museum at **Earle Hill Head Farm** for the past 15 years. Exhibits include farm equipment, household utensils and items of memorabilia from a bygone agricultural era. Please telephone (0668) 81243 for details of opening hours.

Mrs Armstrong also provides accommodation at the 2,500-acre working farm. Bed and breakfast is available at the farmhouse (one twin and two double rooms), and high quality, self-catering accommodation at nearby Firwood House, a handsome Vitorian bungalow with fine views of Glendale and the Cheviots. The building has been tastefully divided into two fully-equipped holiday houses, each accommodating six to nine people.

It's worth walking across the fells (a high-level footpath runs from

Wooler) or, for the less energetic, travelling along the A697 and B6351 westwards from Wooler to **Kirknewton**. This typical border village of cottages, school and village church could not seem more peaceful. But at Old Yeavering, one-and-a-half-miles to the east, stands a great stone in the field which marks the spot where, in 1415, Robert Umfraville, a Northumbrian hero, put to flight 4,000 Scottish troops with a force of only 600 men.

In the Kirknewton churchyard is evidence of a more recent conflict, the graves, near the church gate, of young pilots from nearby RAF Millfield. In another corner are those of four young German airmen who died in the same conflict in 1943. Also buried here is Josephine Butler, the great Victorian social reformer and fighter for women's rights, who retired to Northumberland and died here in 1906. An unusual medieval sculpture in the church shows the Magi wearing kilts - a fascinating example of medieval artists presenting the Christian story in ways their audience could understand.

Barely half a mile east of the village, in what are now fields by the little River Glen, once lay the royal township of Gefrin or Ad-Gefrin. This huge settlement of timber-framed buildings, including halls 100ft long and a great amphitheatre, was the capital of Edwin, the first Christian King of Northumbria. The great historian, Bede, recalls that it was here, in 627AD, that St Paulinus spent 36 days teaching Christianity to the people of Northumbria and baptising converts in the River Glen. A stone monument now marks the place where this long-vanished town once stood.

If such historical associations were not enough, on the summit of a nearby hill known as Yeavering Bell, there is a magnificent Iron-Age hillfort, the largest in Northumberland, enclosed by the remains of a wall and covering 13 acres. Over 33 hut circles have been traced on the summit, which commands impressive views for miles around.

Doddington, about three miles north of Wooler, lies close to Dodd Law, another area rich in archaeological remains that can be explored on foot. There is a prehistoric hillfort, which continued to be occupied into Roman times, and rocks with extensive Bronze-Age markings. On the south of the summit is Cuddy's Cove which, according to legend, was once occupied by St Cuthbert in his early years as an impoverished, itinerant shepherd-preacher.

Chillingham, south-east of Wooler, is a pleasant village with yet another ruined medieval castle; but it is perhaps best known for the herd of wild, horned, white cattle that roam the 365-acre park. One of only five herds of their kind in Britain, they have survived because of their comparative isolation, and are perhaps the purest surviving specimens of the wild cattle that once roamed the hills and forests of prehistoric Britain.

Belford, to the east, is an attractive town of stone houses whose broad main street contains some interesting, old shops and a fine old coaching inn, reflecting the fact that this was once an important town on the Great North Road. Belford Hall, not open to the public, was designed by the great 18th century architect, James Paine, in an elegant Palladian style.

Belford is in the ideal place for a holiday base. It stands on the edge of the lovely Kyloe Hills with the long golden beaches and rocky outcrops of the coast in sight. The Cheviots, the National Park and the lovely Flodden Field are within easy reach to the west. The historic towns of Berwick and Alnwick, the mystic splendour of the Holy Island of Lindisfarne and the majesty of Bamburgh Castle - Belford is surrounded by them all.

Among the attractions of the village you will find **Belford Craft Gallery** near the Market Cross. Its tea and coffee shop is undoubtedly one of the most popular meeting places - serving the Northumberland speciality of 'Singin' Hinnies' baked on a 'girdle' beside the tables.

The Craft Gallery's visitor centre will be pleased to offer you help and advice about the facilities and attractions of the area.

An impressive display of Belford Pottery produced on the premises by the owner's talented son and daughter-in-law can be found in the craft shop, in addition to many other crafts and paintings by local people, cards, books, Northumberland music and jewellery of Celtic design. Indeed an Aladdin's Cave for visitors, whether you intend to spend a few pence or many pounds, there will be something here to interest you.

Belford Craft Gallery

Noel Bray, the renowned artist of aviation painting, has his studio at the Belford Activity Centre, which offers arts and crafts activity holidays and day courses for those who would like to develop an existing skill or to try something entirely new. There is a wide range of courses, all tutored by talented and experienced craftspersons and tailored to suit individuals of all abilities. The centre offers accommodation and meals, many on-site facilities and transport to and from all location work. Non-residents are welcome, as are caravans, which may be parked on a private site to the rear of the centre.

Noel Bray Studio

The B1342 east of Belford leads to the village of **Waren Mill** and **Budle Bay,** a large inlet of flats and sand where vast numbers of wading birds and wildfowl come to feed. Caution should be taken when walking on the flats, as sections quickly become cut off at high tide.

Waren House is the only four Crown highly commended hotel in Northumbria and is definitely a perfect example of first class accommodation, having recently won an award from the RAC for Overall Comfort.

Situated on the edge of Budle Bay and set in six acres of beautiful woodland and well-maintained gardens, the Hotel offers guests the ideal base to enjoy and explore the delights of North Northumberland and the Scottish borders.

There are five en-suite rooms and two suites, all superbly decorated in differing styles, from Edwardian and Victorian to Oriental and French. All have direct dial telephones, colour TV (including satellite), trouser press, fruit, sweets, hot drinks facilities and mineral water.

Dinner, four courses of traditional English cuisine with extensive choice, is served in the romantic, candlelit dining room overlooking the Bay towards the Holy Island. You will be impressed by the fine selection of over 200 wines to accompany your meal, and by the professional and attentive management and staff who will ensure that your stay at Waren House Hotel is a memorable experience that you will wish to repeat as soon as possible.

The Hotel is not suitable for children or pets. There is no smoking, except cigarettes only in the library.

Waren House Hotel

St Cuthbert's Cave, on the moors about four miles west of Belford and only accessible by track and footpath, is a natural cave concealed by a great overhanging rock. It is believed that the saint's body may have lain here on its much interrupted journey across Northumbria. There are superb views of the coast from the summit of nearby Greensheen Hill.

Heading north from Belford on the A1, watch out for Haggerston Caravan Park on your right. Some three miles further on, take the seaward turning for **Cheswick** village. Here you will find **Ladythorne House**, a beautiful Georgian House built in 1721, now a family bed and breakfast establishment offering accommodation of the highest standard.

Situated between Lindisfarne (Holy Island) and Berwick, it is the ideal base for fishing, walking on sandy beaches and over the Cheviot Hills, and birdwatching at Fenham Flats and Budle Bay.

Val and her husband Rob run Ladythorne House and organise their own fishing trips on their sea-going charter boat, which can accommodate six to twelve persons. Rob and his father, who are builders by trade, have done an excellent job of totally renovating the building, while Val is responsible for the superb interior design. The results are magnificent.

Double, twin-bedded, single-bedded and family rooms are available, and all age groups are welcome.

It is very much a family home with an easy-going, comfortable atmosphere.

Ladythorne House

The road from here will take you to **Goswick,** and just to the south of the village are **Beachcomber Cottages.** These are very much as one might imagine - accommodation situated in an isolated, quiet position on sand-dunes overlooking miles of empty beach, open sea and peaceful country-side.

Sue Marrs and Julie Holden have equipped the two 'fisherman's' cottages and self-contained flat to a high standard for comfortable and convenient self-catering. There is also a small camp site available for tents and touring caravans, and a little bar serving drinks and snacks.

Because of the variety of activities available, this is an ideal place for a family holiday. There is tennis on site and the Goswick Golf Course is just half-a-mile away. Horse riding on the beach and sea fishing are easily arranged. Pets are welcome, if kept under sensible control, for there are long walks along the beach and in the countryside which may be enjoyed with the family dog. Nature lovers are always pleased to discover that the area is excellent for birdwatching.

Beachcomber Cottages

The coastline between Bamburgh and Berwick is as fine as that to the immediate south, though with much more extensive sandbanks. But one feature above all others dominates - **Lindisfarne, or Holy Island.**

You can get across, only at low tide, along the three-mile-long causeway from **Beal** (tide tables are published locally and are displayed at each end of the road - there are refuges part way for those who fail to time it correctly) or by regular service bus from Berwick, which has a 'tide' rather than a 'time' table. As you cross, note the 11th century Pilgrims Way, marked by stakes, still visible about 200 yards south of the modern causeway. This route was in use until comparatively recent times.

Holy Island

This most evocative of English islands was known as Lindisfarne until the 11th century when a group of Benedictine monks settled here, giving it the name Holy Island. Both names are now used. The ruins of their great sandstone priory, in massive Romanesque style with great pillars, can still be explored.

But the links with early Christianity are even more significant than that of the Benedictines, for it was here, in 635AD, that St Aidan and his small community of Irish monks came from Iona to found a base from which to help convert northern England to Christianity. This can truly be said to be one of the cradles of English Christianity.

The monks are also remembered for having produced some of the finest surviving examples of Celtic art, the richly decorated Lindisfarne Gospels, which were commenced in the 7th century. When the island was invaded by Vikings in the 9th century, the monks fled, taking their precious gospels with them. These have, miraculously, survived and are now in the safety of the British Museum. Facsimiles are kept on Lindisfarne and can be seen in the 12th century parish church on the island. Only a few carved stones remain from the original monastic buildings.

St Cuthbert also came here, living on a tiny islet as a hermit before seeking even further seclusion on the Farne Islands. A cross marks the site of his tiny chapel, which can be reached over the sand and rocks at low tide.

Lindisfarne Castle was established in Tudor times as yet another fortification to protect the exposed flank of Northumbria from invasion by the Scots. It was extensively rebuilt and restored in 1903 as a private house by the great Edwardian architect, Edward Lutyens, and is now in the care of the National Trust. It is open, with its small walled garden, to the public during the summer months.

The third Manor House to be built on Holy Island was built about 150 years ago, and this is now the **Manor House Hotel.** Sitting in the market square, this fine building offers uninterrupted views of the harbour and Lindisfarne Castle.

Manor House Hotel

Run by resident proprietors George and Jennifer Ward, the hotel has 10 bedrooms, nine of which offer en-suite facilities. All rooms have colour television and tea making facilities, and George and Jennifer intend to make life easier for their disabled guests by installing a stair lift.

The 32-cover restaurant at the Manor House is open seven nights a week and is also popular with non-residents. Dine from the full a la carte menu, or - should you be there on a Sunday evening - you can enjoy that old traditional favourite, roast beef and yorkshire pudding. Vegetarians are well looked after and can choose from a separate menu. Bar meals are available every day, both lunchtime and evening.

Active guets will perhaps wish to indulge in some sea fishing - trips can easily be arranged. Alternatively, a walk around the island is an excellent opportunity to explore the beaches and sand dunes, or you may simply enjoy relaxing in the Hotel's comfy lounge bar.

Most visitors to the Manor House Hotel come here for the same reasons - to enjoy a family holiday in a family atmosphere in quiet and restful surroundings.

If what you're longing for is a real 'get away from it all' break, then Judith James appears to have the answer for you on Holy Island.

Judith owns the **North View Lodge** guest house, and although a warm welcome is extended to everyone, she particularly caters for people who enjoy a degree of isolation, whether it be for one night, or a week or more.

North View Lodge is over 400 years old and is reputed to be the oldest house on this historic island, which is surrounded by water twice daily. There are three guest bedrooms available all year round, all of which have en-suite facilities. A traditional breakfast is served each morning and Judith offers anything from fish and chips to a full a la carte menu in the evenings. North View Lodge is licensed, so there is the added bonus of being able to enjoy a drink with your meal.

North View Lodge undoubtedly offers excellent value for money, although it is advisable to telephone before arriving - particularly in the high season. Holy Island is very popular with visitors - especially escapologists!

Holy Island village is a community of around 170 people who work in farming, in the island's distillery (noted for excellent traditional mead and strong liquors) and in the tourist trade. Much of the island is also a Nature Reserve, with wildflowers and a wide variety of seabirds. You can look back to the mainland or out across the North Sea and, at least for a few moments, share the sense of peace and tranquillity that Aidan and Cuthbert also knew along this beautiful coastline.

North View Lodge

St Marys Island

Reference Guide

to

Hotels, Guest Houses, Inns, Public Houses,

Self Catering Accommodation, Farm Accommodation,

Caravan and Camping Parks, Restaurants,

Riding Schools and Places of Interest

Details in this section are for guidance only.

For more information please contact the individual establishments

who will be only too pleased to help.

Chapter 1 : Cleveland

Inns & Public Houses

Name & Address	Telephone No	Page No
Leo's Pub Club Redcar Cleveland	0642 487999	13

Hotels & Guest Houses

Name & Address	Telephone No	Page No
Claxton Hotel 196 High Street Redcar Cleveland TS10 3AW	0642 486745	14
Golden Eagle Hotel Trenchard Avenue Thornaby-on-Tees Cleveland TS17 ODA	0642 766511	8
The Grand Hotel Swainson Street Hartlepool TS24 8AA	0429 266345	21
Norman Conquest Hotel Flatts Lane Normanby Middlesborough	O642 454333	12
Sheraton Hotel 37 Yarm Road Stockton on Tees Cleveland TS18 3NP	674211 618655	9

Chapter 1 : Cleveland - Continued

Hotels & Guest Houses

Name & Address	Telephone No	Page No
The Southern Cross Dixons Bank Marton Middlesborough TS2 1AA	0642 317539	13

Restaurants

Name & Address	Telephone No	Page No
Norman Conquest Hotel Flatts Lane Normanby Middlesborough	O642 454333	12

Self Catering Accommodation

Name & Address	Telephone No	Page No
Highcliffe Cottage C/O Street House Farm Loftus Saltburn Cleveland	0287 40541	18

Farmhouse Accommodation

Name & Address	Telephone No	Page No
Maltby Farm Maltby Middelsborough Cleveland TS8 OBP	0642 590121	10

Chapter 1 : Cleveland - Continued

Places of Interest

Name & Address	Telephone No	Page No
Castle Eden Walk C/O Cleveland County Council PO Box 100a Municiple Buildings Middlesborough	0642 248155	19
Kirkleatham Hall Museum Krikleatham Redcar Cleveland TS10 5NW	0642 479500	15
Leven Close Farm High Leven Nr Yarm Cleveland TS15 9JP	0642 750114	11

Chapter Two : Central Durham

Inns & Public Houses

Name & Address	Telephone No	Page No
Hat & Feather Medomsley Consett Co Durham DH8 6RD	0207 504210	35

Hotels & Guest Houses

Name & Address	Telephone No	Page No
Adolphus 14 Adolphus Street West Seaham Co Durham SR7 7SE	091 581 6746	51
Castledene 37 Nevilledale Terrace Durham DH1 4QG	091 384 8386	29
Crown & Crossed Swords Front Street Shotley Bridge Co Durham DH8 OHU	0207 502006	34
Dunvegan B&B Darlington Road Merryoaks Durham DH1 3PR	091 384 4568	30
Mount Pleasant Hotel 23 New Market Street Consett Co Durham	0207 502526	32

Chapter Two : Central Durham - Continued

Hotels & Guest Houses

Name & Address	Telephone No	Page No
Oak Tree Inn Hotel **Tantobie** **Nr Stanley** **Co Durham DH9 9RF**	**0207 235455**	**37**
Old Manor House Hotel **The Green** **West Auckland** **Durham DL14 9HW**	**0388 834834**	**47**
Park Head Hotel **New Coundon** **Bishop Auckland** **Co Durham**	**0388 661727**	**45**
Pondfield Villa **Rowley** **Consett** **Co Durham DH8 9HF**	**0207 508354**	**33**
The Uplands Hotel **Acacia Gardens** **Crook** **Co Durham DL15 9NB**	**0388 762539**	**49**
Walworth Castle Hotel **Walworth** **Darlington** **Co Durham DL2 2LY**	**0325 485470**	**39**

Chapter Two : Central Durham - Continued

Farmhouse Accommodation

Name & Address	Telephone No	Page No
Waldridge Hall Farm Old Waldridge Chester Le Street Co Durham DH2 3SL	091 388 4210	38

Restaurants

Name & Address	Telephone No	Page No
Crombies Restaurant 36/44 Tubwell Row Darlington Co Durham DL1 1PD	0325 464475	40

Places of Interest

Name & Address	Telephone No	Page No
Bernhardt Gallery 60 Coniscliffe Road Darlington Co Durham DL3 7RN	0325 356633	41
Bygones Antiques 3/5 McCullen Road Darlington DL1 1BW	0325 461399	42
Leap Mill Farm Burnopfield Co Durham NE16 6BJ	0207 71375	36
Tanfield Railway Durham County Council County Hall, Durham DH1 5UQ	091 386 4411	31

Chapter Three : Teesdale

Inns & Public Houses

Name & Address	Telephone No	Page No
The Ancient Unicorn Inn Bowes Barnard Castle DL2 9HN	0833 28321	67
The Red Well Inn Harmire Road Barnard Castle Co Durham DL12 8QS	0833 37002	59

Hotels & Guest Houses

Name & Address	Telephone No	Page No
Brunswick House Market Place Middleton in Teesdale Co Durham DL12 OQH	0833 40393	74
The Coach House Whorlton Nr Barnard Castle Co Durham DL12 8XQ	0833 27237	64
Gazebo House 4 North Green Staindrop Co Durham DL2 3JN	0833 60222	62
Holme House Piercebridge Darlington DL2 3SY	0325 374280	66

Chapter Three : Teesdale - Continued

Hotels & Guest Houses

Name & Address	Telephone No	Page No
Low Green Mickleton Barnard Castle, Co Durham	0833 40425	70
Quakers Rest 20 North Green Staindrop, Darlington Co Durham DL2 3NJ	0833 60669	62
The Red Well Inn Harmire Road Barnard Castle Co Durham DL12 8QS	0833 37002	59
Teesdale Hotel Market Square Middleton in Teesdale DL12 OQG	0833 40264	72

Restaurants

Name & Address	Telephone No	Page No
Brunswick House Market Place Middleton in Teesdale Co Durham DL12 OQH	0833 40393	73

Self Catering Accommodation

Name & Address	Telephone No	Page No
Brock Scar Cottage Brock Scar Farm Kelton Middleton in Teesdale DL12 OPW	0833 40495	71

Chapter Three : Teesdale - Continued

Self Catering Accommodation

Name & Address	Telephone No	Page No
Park End Farm Holwick Nr Middleton in Teesdale Co Durham	0833 40261	76
The Shooting Lodge High Shipley Farm Egglestone Barnard Castle Co Durham	0833 37024	68
Thwaite Hall Cotherstone Barnard Castle Co Durham DL12 9UQ	0833 50782	67

Farmhouse Accommodation

Name & Address	Telephone No	Page No
Snailsgill Farm Middleton in Teesdale Barnard Castle Co Durham DL12 ORP	0833 40343	75

Caravan & Camping Parks

Name & Address	Telephone No	Page No
Hetherick Caravan Park Marwood Barnard Castle Co Durham DL12 8QX	0833 31170	60

Chapter Three : Teesdale - Continued

Caravan & Camping Parks

Name & Address	Telephone No	Page No
Mickleton Mill Caravan Park Mickleton Barnard Castle Co Durham DL12 OLS	0833 40317	70

Places of Interest

Name & Address	Telephone No	Page No
The Bowes Museum Barnard Castle Co Durham DL12 8NP	0833 690606	58

Chapter Four : Weardale

Inns & Public Houses

Name & Address	Telephone No	Page No
The Pack Horse Inn 8 Market Place Stanhope Bishop Auckland Co Durham DL13 2UJ	0388 528407	92
Rookhope Inn Rookhope Bishop Auckland Weardale	0388 517215	90

Hotels & Guest Houses

Name & Address	Telephone No	Page No
The Bonny Moor Hen Front Street Stanhope Co Durham DL13 2TS	0388 528214	91
Heatherside B&B Edmundbyers Co Durham DH8 9NL	0207 55674	97
Westgate Guest House Westgate in Weardale Bishop Auckland Co Durham DL13 1LW	0388 517564	88

Self Catering Accommodation

Name & Address	Telephone No	Page No
Daleview Holiday Flats St Johns Chapel Weardale Co Durham DL13 1QF	0388 537231	87
Thistlewood Cottage Thistlewood Hall Thistlewood Lane Wolsingham Bishop Auckland Co Durham	0388 527304	95

Farmhouse Accommodation

Name & Address	Telephone No	Page No
Friarside Farm Wolsingham Weardale DL13 3BH	0388 527361	94
Lands Farm Westgate in Weardale Bishop Auckland Co Durham	0388 517210	89

Riding Schools

Name & Address	Telephone No	Page No
Alston & Killhope Riding Centre Low Cornriggs Farm Cowshill Wearside CoDurham DL13 1AQ	0388 537600	85

Chapter Four : Weardale - Continued
Places of Interest

Name & Address	Telephone No	Page No
Hamsterly Forest Forestry Commission Redford Hamsterly Bishop Auckland Co Durham DL13 3NL	0388 88312	95
Killhope Wheel Lead Mining Centre Durham County Council Environment Department County Hall Durham DH1 5UQ	091 386 4411	84

Chapter Five : Tyneside

Hotels & Guest Houses

Name & Address	Telephone No	Page No
Aydon Grange Corbridge Northumberland NE45 5PW	091 281 8430	120
The Beaumont Hotel Beaumont Street Hexham Northumberland NE46 3LT	0434 602331	116
Crowberry Hall Allendale Hexham Northumberland NE47 9SR	0434 683392	112
Hotspur Hotel Allendale Hexham Northumberland NE47 9BW	0434 683355	113
Vallum Lodge Hotel Military Road Twice Brewed Bardon Mill Northumberland NE47 7AN	0434 344248	104
White Lion Hotel High Cross Street Brampton Cumbria	06977 2338	110

Chapter Five : Tyneside - Continued

Hotels & Guest Houses

Name & Address	Telephone No	Page No
Rye Hill Farm Slaley Hexham Northumberland NE47 OAH	0434 673259	121

Self Catering Accommodation

Name & Address	Telephone No	Page No
Rye Hill Farm Country Holidays Slaley Hexham Northumberland NE47 OAH	0434 673259	121

Farmhouse Accommodation

Name & Address	Telephone No	Page No
Burnt Walls Greenhead Northumberland CAG 7HX	06972 272	105
Oaky Knowe Farm Haltwistle Northumberland NE49 ONB	0434 320648	111
Holmehead Farm Hadrian's Wall Greenhead Via Carlisle Northumberland CAG 74Y	06972 402	107

Chapter Five : Tyneside - Continued

Caravan & Camping Parks

Name & Address	Telephone No	Page No
Riverside Leisure Tyne Green Hexham Northumberland NE46 3RY	0434 604705	117

Places of Interest

Name & Address	Telephone No	Page No
Goodies at Gresham House Watling Street Corbridge Northumberland NE45 5AH	0434 632557	119
New Mills Trout Farm Brampton Cumbria CA8 2QS	06977 2384	

Chapter Six : Tyneside

Inns & Public Houses

Name & Address	Telephone No	Page No
Bridge End Inn Ovingham Prudhoe NE42 6BN	0661 32219	127
Holiday Inn Seaton Burn Great North Road Newcastle NE13 6BP	091 236 5432	133

Hotels & Guest Houses

Name & Address	Telephone No	Page No
The Wheatsheaf Hotel Callerton Lane Ends Woolsington Nr Newcastle	091 286 9254	135

Places of Interest

Name & Address	Telephone No	Page No
Gateshead Parks Recreation Dept Prince Consort Road Gateshead Tyne & Wear NE8 4HJ	4901616	136

Chapter Seven : Central Northumberland

Inns & Public Houses

Name & Address	Telephone No	Page No
The Anglers Arms Weldon Bridge Long Framlington Northumberland NE65 8AX	0665 570655	155
Bay Horse Inn West Woodburn Hexham Northumberland NE48 2RX	0434 270218	150
Bird in Bush Inn Elsdon Nr Otterburn Northumberland NE19 1AA	0830 20478	159
The Tone Inn on A68 Nr Birtley Hexham Northumberland NE48 3JQ	0434 270417	151
The Salmon Inn Holystone Sharperton Morpeth NE65 7AJ	0669 50285	153

Chapter Seven : Central Northumberland - Continued

Hotels & Guest Houses

Name & Address	Telephone No	Page No
Breamish House Hotel Powburn Nr Alnwick Northumberland NE66 4LL	066578 266	161
Newcastle Hotel Front Street Rothbury Northumberland NE65 7UT	0669 20334	154
Ogle House Eglingham Village Alnwick Northumberland NE66 2TZ	0665 78264	162
Old Post Office Cottage Little Bavington Capheaton Northumberland NE19 2BB	0830 30331	160
Ravenshill Kielder Northumberland NE48 1EL	0434 250251	147
Thorneyburn Lodge Tarset Northumberland NE48 1NA	0434 240272	

Self Catering Accommodation

Name & Address	Telephone No	Page No
Roseden Wooperton Alnwick NE66 4XU	06687 271	163

Restaurants

Name & Address	Telephone No	Page No
Ogle House Eglingham Village Alnwick Northumberland NE66 2TZ	0665 78264	162
Kielder Water Restaurant Tower Knowe Yarrow Moor Falstone Hexham NE48 1BH	0660 240400	146
Ravenshill Kielder Northumberland NE48 1EL	0434 250251	147

Places of Interest

Name & Address	Telephone No	Page No
Kielder Bikes Hawkhope Car Park Kielder Water NE48 1BX	0434 220392	147
Otterburn Mill Showroom Otterburn Northumberland NE19 1JT	0830 20225	157

Chapter Eight : The Northumberland Coast

Hotels & Guest Houses

Name & Address	Telephone No	Page No
Bamburgh Castle Hotel Seahouses Northumberland NE68 7SQ	0665 720283	185
Dunstan Hill Farm Embleton Northumberland NE66 3TQ	066576 481	179
Lakeside Hotel Woodhorn Village Ashington Northumberland NE63 9AT	0670 862001	171
The Links Hotel 8 Kings Street Seahouses Northumberland NE68 7XP	0665 720062	184
North Cottage Birling Warkworth Northumberland NE65 OXS	0665 711 263	176
The Oaks Hotel South Road Alnwick Northumberland NE66 2PN	0665 510014	178

Chapter Eight : The Northumberland Coast- Continued

Hotels & Guest Houses

Name & Address	Telephone No	Page No
Beach House Hotel Seafront Seahouses Northumberland NE68 7SR	0665 720337	183
The Olde Ship Hotel 9 Main Street Seahouses Northumberland NE68 7RD	0665 720200	182
Warkworth House Hotel 16 Bridge Street Warkworth Northumberland NE65 OXB	0665 711276	175

Restaurants & Tea Rooms

Name & Address	Telephone No	Page No
Borgias Restaurant 108a Front Street East Bedlington Nr Blythe	0670 822338	170
Copper Kettle 21 Front Street Bamburgh NE69 7BW	06684 315	187
Giannis Pizzeria 3 Market Place Morpeth Northumberland NE61 1HG	0670 511547	173

Places of Interest

Name & Address	Telephone No	Page No
Norselands Gallery Studio 2 The Old School Warrenford Nr Belford Northumberland	0668 213465	189
Northumbria Crafts 5 Main Street Seahouses Northumberland NE68 7RD	0665 720890	184

Chapter Nine : Berwick & The Border

Inns & Public Houses

Name & Address	Telephone No	Page No
Fishers Arms Horncliffe Berwick upon Tweed Northumberland TD15 2XW	0289 86223	202
The Galleon 50 Main Steet Spittal Berwick upon Tweed TD15 1QY	0289 305560	200
The Meadow House Great North Road Berwick upon Tweed TD15 1UR	0289 304173	198
Red Lion Hotel 1 High Street Wooler NE71 6LB	0668 81629	204
Tankerville Arms Hotel Wooler Northumberland NE71 6AD	0668 81581	206

Hotels & Guest Houses

Name & Address	Telephone No	Page No
Ladythorne House Cheswick Berwick upon Tweed Northumberland	0289 87282	211

Hotels & Guest Houses

Name & Address	Telephone No	Page No
Loreto Guest House 1 Rycroft Way Wooler Northumberland	0668 81350	206
The Manor House Hotel Holy Island Berwick upon Tweed Northumberland	0289 89207	215
Meadow Hill House Duns Road Berwick upon Tweed Northumberland TD15 1TN	0289 306325	198
North View Lodge Marygate Holy Island Northumberland TD15 1SD	0289 89222	216
Warren House Hotel Warren Mill Belford Northumberland NE70 7EE	06684 581	210

Self Catering Accommodation

Name & Address	Telephone No	Page No
Beachcomber Cottages Beachcomber House Goswick Northumberland TD15 2RW	0289 81217	212

Farmhouse Accommodation

Name & Address	Telephone No	Page No
Middle Ord Farm Berwick upon Tweed TD15 2XQ	0289 306323	201
Earle Hill Head Farm Earle Hill Wooler Northumberland	0668 81243	207

Restaurants

Name & Address	Telephone No	Page No
The Rob Roy Dock Road Tweedmouth Berwick upon Tweed TD15 2BQ	0289 306428	199

Places of Interest

Name & Address	Telephone No	Page No
Belford Craft Gallery Market Place Belford Northumberland NE70 7ND	0668 213888	209
Berwick Borough Council Council Offices Wallace Green Berwick upon Tweed TD15 1ED	0289 330044	196

Places of Interest

Name & Address	Telephone No	Page No
Earle Hill Head Farm Earle Hill Wooler Northumberland	0668 81243	207
Noel Bray Studio 7-9 West Street Belford Northumberland NE70 7QA	0668 213486	210

THE HIDDEN PLACES

If you would like to have any of the titles currently available in this series, please complete this coupon and send to:

M & M Publishing Ltd
Tryfan House, Warwick Drive
Hale, Altrincham
Cheshire, WA15 9EA

Somerset, Avon and Dorset	☐	£ 5.90 inc. p&p
Norfolk and Suffolk	☐	£ 5.90 inc. p&p
Yorkshire South, East andWest	☐	£ 5.90 inc. p&p
Devon and Cornwall	☐	£ 5.90 inc. p&p
North Yorkshire	☐	£ 5.90 inc. p&p
Cumbria	☐	£ 5.90 inc. p&p
Southern and Central Scotland	☐	£ 5.90 inc. p&p
Sussex	☐	£ 5.90 inc. p&p
Hampshire and the Isle of Wight	☐	£ 5.90 inc. p&p
Gloucestershire & Wiltshire	☐	£ 5.90 inc. p&p
Nottinghamshire, Derbyshire & Lincolnshire	☐	£ 5.90 inc. p&p
Oxfordshire, Buckinghamshire & Bedfordshire	☐	£ 5.90 inc. p&p
Lancashire & Cheshire	☐	£ 5.90 inc. p&p
Hereford & Worcester	☐	£ 5.90 inc. p&p
Set of any Five	☐	£ 25.90 inc. p&p

NAME...

ADDRESS..

....

...............................Post Code...

Please make cheques/postal orders payable to: M & M Publishing Ltd